DUNNE & CRESCENZI

The Menu

Selected and edited by

EILEEN DUNNE CRESCENZI

Photography by

FEDERICA CRESCENZI

MERCIER PRESS
IRISH PUBLISHER – IRISH STORY

This book is dedicated
to our customers
who have supported us
through the years.

MERCIER PRESS
Cork
www.mercierpress.ie

© Eileen Dunne Crescenzi, 2011

Photography by Federica Crescenzi

ISBN: 978 1 85635 881 1

10 9 8 7 6 5 4 3 2 1

A CIP record for this title is available from the British Library

Printed and bound in the EU.

The Menu

Antipasti

Grilled Mediterranean vegetables
Delizie dell'orto ... 27

Campania buffalo mozzarella, aubergine and prawn stack
Millefoglie di bufala di Campania con gamberi, melanzane e pesto ... 29

Bresaola from Valtellina, rocket and parmigiano
Bresaola di Valtellina, rughetta e parmigiano ... 31

Portobello mushrooms with Gorgonzola and pesto stuffing
Funghi ripieni di Gorgonzola e pesto ... 33

Smoked Irish salmon with avocado, goat's cheese and rocket
Rotolini di salmone irlandese affumicato con avocado, caprino e rughetta ... 35

Campania buffalo mozzarella with grilled peppers and fresh basil
Mozzarella di bufala di Campania con peperoni grigliati e basilico ... 37

Prosciutto San Daniele with baby spinach,
Grana Trentino cheese shavings and radicchio
*Prosciutto San Daniele con insalatina di spinaci,
scaglie di Grana Trentino e radicchio ... 39*

Sauté of mussels
Sauté di cozze ... 41

Speck and Asiago polenta crostini
Crostini di polenta di speck e Asiago ... 43

Polenta and spinach crostini
Crostini di polenta con spinaci ... 43

Bruschetta with fresh vine-ripened tomatoes and basil
Bruschetta con pomodoro e basilico ... 45

Bruschetta with mushrooms and ricotta bows
Bruschetta con funghi misti e fiocchi di ricotta ... 47

Bruschetta with tuna, olives, capers and sun-dried tomatoes
Bruschetta con tonno, olive, capperi e pomodori secchi ... 49

Baked crostini with anchovies, Prosciutto di Parma, parmigiano and rocket
Crostini caldi dal forno ... 51

Bruschetta with borlotti beans and tomato
Bruschetta con fagioli e salsa di pomodoro ... 52

Soups

Minestrone soup
Minestrone ... 59

Borlotti bean soup
Zuppa di fagioli ... 61

Butternut squash, scallop and almond soup
Crema di zucca, mandorle e capesante ... 63

Chickpea soup with pasta
Zuppa di ceci ... 64

Lentil and mussel soup
Zuppa di lenticchie e cozze ... 65

Pea, prawn and mint soup
Vellutata di piselli e menta con gamberi ... 67

Salads

Gaeta olive salad
Insalata Gaeta ... 71

Warm chicken salad with pancetta and peppers
Insalata di pollo con pancetta e peperoni ... 73

Warm goat's cheese salad with William pear and walnuts
Insalata del Pastore ... 75

Orange and fennel salad
Insalata di arancio con finocchio e olive ... 77

Puntarelle with anchovy sauce
Puntarelle con salsa di acciughe ... 79

Marche Bomba salad
Insalata bomba ... 81

Pasta & Risotto

Ravioli with ricotta and spinach
Ravioli con ricotta e spinaci ... 89

Ravioli with smoked Irish salmon and orange zest
Ravioli con salmone irlandese affumicato con arancio ... 90

Spinach and ricotta tortelli with parmigiano cream and balsamic reduction
Tortelli di ricotta e spinaci con fonduta di parmigiano e riduzione di balsamico ... 91

Dunne & Crescenzi pasta with tomato and basil sauce
Spaghetti al pomodoro e basilico ... 93

Squid ink pasta with fruits of the sea
Linguine al nero di seppia ai frutti di mare ... 95

Strozzapreti with aubergines, pine nuts, speck and cherry tomatoes
Strozzapreti con melanzane, pinoli, speck e pomodorini ... 97

Fettuccine with salmon and courgette
Fettuccine con salmone e zucchine ... 99

Bucatini pasta with guanciale and tomato
Bucatini all'amatriciana ... 101

Paccheri pasta from Gragnano with Dublin Bay prawns and tomato
Paccheri di Gragnano con gamberi e pomodoro ... 103

Pappardelle with duck and vinsanto
Pappardelle con anatra profumate al vinsanto ... 105

Penne with tomato, garlic and chilli
Penne all'arrabbiata ... 107

Rigatoni alla carbonara
Rigatoni alla carbonara ... 109

Risotto with red cabbage and robiola cheese
Risotto al cavolo rosso e robiola ... 140

Risotto with grappa, quail, saffron and radicchio
Risotto alla grappa con petti di quaglia, zafferano e radicchio ... 141

Risotto with cream of scampi
Risotto alla crema di scampi ... 143

Risotto with fruits of the sea
Risotto ai frutti di mare ... 144

Risotto with scallops and fennel
Risotto con scaglie di capesante e finocchio ... 145

Risotto with radicchio, Gorgonzola and walnuts
Risotto con radicchio, Gorgonzola e noci ... 147

Risotto with butternut squash, speck and Grana Trentino
Risotto con zucca, speck e Grana Trentino ... 148

Risotto with Barolo
Risotto al Barolo ... 149

Risotto with cream of asparagus and Pecorino
Risotto con crema di asparagi e Pecorino ... 151

Main Courses

Pan-fried hake with cherry tomatoes
Nasello in padella sul letto di pomodorini ... 155

Calamari filled with ricotta and pistachio nuts from Bronte
Calamari ripieni di ricotta e pistacchi di Bronte ... 157

Sicilian Couscous
Cuscusu Siciliano ... 159

King prawns with citrus and zibibbo sauce
Mazzancolle con salsa di agrumi e zibibbo ... 161

Parcels of Irish salmon with citrus sauce
Filetto di salmone irlandese in cartoccio con salsa di agrumi ... 163

Fish parcels with cherry tomatoes, capers and olives
Pesce in cartoccio con pomodorini, capperi e olive ... 165

Sea bass with black olive and potato crust
Spigola in crosta di olive nere e patate ... 167

Squid, peas and potato stew
Calamari con patate e piselli ... 169

Pot-roasted rabbit
Coniglio alla cacciatora ... 171

Veal liver with shallots, Venetian style
Fegato alla Veneziana ... 173

Sienese sausage and bean casserole
Salsiccia con fagioli ... 175

Twice-cooked polpette
Polpette ripassate in padella ... 176

Veal steaks with prosciutto and sage
Saltimbocca ... 179

Chicken roulade with mortadella, spinach and pine nuts
Involtini di pollo con mortadella, spinaci e pinoli ... 181

Chicken with yellow peppers and black olives
Pollo con peperoni gialli e olive nere ... 183

Braised lamb shanks with balsamic and red wine reduction
Stracotto di agnello al forno con riduzione di vino rosso e balsamico ... 185

Fillet of pork with porcini and truffle stuffing, and balsamic reduction
Filetto di maiale ripieno con funghi porcini e tartufo e riduzione balsamico ... 186

Rosemary grilled lamb cutlets
Agnello scottadito ... 189

Fillet of organic Irish beef with red wine reduction, parmigiano petals and rocket
Filetto di manzo biologico irlandese con una riduzione di vino rosso, petali di parmigiano e rughetta ... 191

Tripe with tomato, mint and Pecorino
Trippa alla Romana ... 193

Polenta with mushrooms and Gorgonzola
Polenta con funghi e Gorgonzola ... 195

Polenta with Italian sausage and pork ribs
Polenta con salsicce e spuntature ... 197

Side Dishes

Braised artichokes
Carciofi alla romana ... 201

Braised vegetables
Verdure brasate ... 201

Spinach with cream of parmigiano
Spinaci con crema di parmigiano ... 202

String beans with balsamic dressing
Fagiolini con balsamico ... 203

Brussel sprouts with leeks, rosemary and speck
Cavoli di Bruxelles con porri, rosmarino e speck ... 203

Carrots with cream of parmigiano
Carote con crema di parmigiano ... 203

Chilli and garlic spinach
Spinaci aglio, olio e peperoncino ... 204

Courgettes with leeks, raisins and pine nuts
Zucchine con porri, uvetta e pinoli ... 204

Mushrooms with garlic and parsley
Funghi trifolati ... 204

Peas with leek, pancetta and mint
Piselli con porri, pancetta e menta ... 205

Red cabbage with Teroldego wine sauce
Cavolo rosso con salsa di vino Teroldego ... 206

Refried broccoli
Broccoli ripassati in padella ... 207

Truffled potatoes
Patate con tartufo ... 207

Rosemary roast potatoes
Patate arrosto con rosmarino ... 207

Pan-fried peppers
Peperonata ... 208

Borlotti or cannellini beans
Fagioli borlotti o cannellini ... 209

Chickpeas
Ceci ... 209

Chilli and garlic lentils
Lenticchie stile marchigiana ... 210

Cream of broad beans with chilli oil
Crema di fave con olio di peperoncino ... 210

Desserts

Tiramisù with vinsanto
Tiramisù al vinsanto ... 215

Ricotta and amarene cherry tart
Torta di ricotta e amarene ... 217

Rich chocolate cake from Capri
Torta Caprese ... 219

Limoncello and peach cake
Torta con le pesche e limoncello ... 221

Pannacotta with fruits of the forest
Pannacotta con frutti di bosco ... 223

Dark chocolate, pear and ricotta cake
Torta di ricotta, pera e cioccolata ... 225

Foreword

Back in 1999, South Frederick Street, where I have lived for many years, was a much less sophisticated street than it is today. So you might imagine my curiosity when the old hairdresser's shop beside my house was carefully painted an unusual shade of purple.

Imagine, if you will, my surprise when the legend 'Dunne & Crescenzi', an odd combination of names, appeared above the shop. I could make no sense of it!

Now imagine my delight when I saw cases and cases of wine being unloaded on the pavement outside. A picture of the future began to emerge.

The shop opened and soon I ventured inside. There I saw a wonderland of unusual and exotic foods and provisions laid out on tables with shelf after shelf of red and green bottles of rich Italian wine. How very convenient, I thought!

Within weeks, bruschettas and salads became available, served on colourful waxed paper. I had never seen that before.

After some months, it was not unusual to see a queue outside the door of Dunne & Crescenzi's. Soon the old locksmith's shop next door to it was painted purple and the two were joined. Purple awnings appeared and tables were laid on the pavement outside. Exotic-looking Italian waiters and waitresses were kept busy serving the growing queues. A third shop was added and the street was transformed.

Over the years, as I watched matters evolve, I began to realise that I was observing the creation of a work of art! To add to my delight it was created with all the necessary ingredients for a masterpiece: colour, passion, skill, intuition, invention and courage, but above all, simplicity and a lack of pretension.

Now, on my street, there is a purple monument to the wonderful cuisine and culture of Italy. It is a meeting place for Irish and Italians alike, with an international reputation.

Eileen's recipes will surely show you how to create your own culinary masterpieces.

As for me, I just have to go next door!

Buon appetito,

Graham Knuttel

Introduction

From time to time it would come up in conversation. Eileen and I would dream of taking some time off and retreating to a small Italian medieval village forgotten by time to recount our amazing experiences to date and what we have learned in the fast-paced, ever-changing world of restaurants.

Whether by design or not, Dunne & Crescenzi has come to represent a particular way of life, of eating and of socialising with friends and family. It has evolved into that which goes beyond the mere business of food service into what can only be described as a *puro punto d'incontro*, quite simply a meeting place, a place of retreat, in which the most Italian of things occurs: socialising and food become inextricably interlinked. And in this respect we feel we have lost ownership of the restaurant. It has become a place of the people, made by the people who so joyously inhabit it.

Over the years it has become a reference point for Italian cuisine, thanks to the many regulars returning day after day, week after week, year after year.

We always try to change, vary and, as a result, grow in line with our customers' expectations. In this respect, Italian cooking is very much alive and adaptive. This can be attributed to the solid foundations upon which Italian cooking is based: a respect for the varied traditional cooking methods and a good understanding of flavour combinations. This is why, over the years, we have been able to cook thousands of different 'Specials of the Day', whose Italian authenticity derives not from the name of a dish, but rather from a profound understanding and respect for the aforementioned basics of Italian cooking. Time has also given us the opportunity to work and re-work what have now become our signature dishes, which vary from the simple *bruschetta con pomodoro* to squid ink pasta with fruits of the sea.

Every morning, armed with a pot of tea or cup of coffee, we discuss what dishes

Introduzione

Ce lo siamo detto e ridetto, dobbiamo scrivere un libro, qualcosa che non sia solo commerciale ma dia il senso ha quello che abbiamo fatto.

Non volendo, o volendo, Dunne & Crescenzi è divenuto un modo di vivere, di mangiare, di incontrarsi con amici, parenti, o per festeggiare un compleanno o un luogo di puro incontro.

È divenuto nel corso degli anni, per chi ci ha seguito fin dall'inizio, via via un punto di riferimento della cucina italiana.

La cucina italiana è estremamente viva perché, fatto salvo l'uso e il rispetto della metodologia di cottura e dei suoi abbinamenti, riesce ad avere infinite combinazioni.

Ecco perché oltre ai piatti che ci hanno contraddistinto e ci hanno permesso di creare un vero e proprio trend, a Dublino, siamo riusciti a sfornare migliaia di piatti del giorno o speciali che altro non erano che combinazioni culinarie di tipo italiano.

Ogni mattina, con il tè o il caffè, insieme ai cuochi che si sono susseguiti alla guida delle nostre cucine, nel corso degli anni, abbiamo discusso i piatti migliori da presentarvi, quelli stagionali, quelli regionali, quelli che davano più senso al tempo metereologico sulla strada e quelli che lasciavano allo stesso cuoco un margine importante della sua creatività ...

Questo continuo essere li, discutere, preparare e presentare, assaggiare è stato per noi un metodo su come dialogare con il nostro cliente da una parte, e percorrere sentieri e tendenze della cucina italiana dall'altra.

I nostri clienti adorano gli speciali! Molti neppure guardano più il menù principale, relegato oramai ad una lista di opzioni per chi non ci conosce o per i turisti o per una cena con gli amici.

Fare questo ci ha permesso anche di

17

to serve with our chefs. We take into account the availability of local seasonal produce, the particulars of the weather of the day and a healthy dose of inspiration from a particular region of Italy, leaving room, of course, for the cook to draw on his or her own creativity. This continuous open-ended process of discussion, preparation, presentation and tasting has become the basis of a dialogue with our customers and a journey exploring the many and diverse tendencies of Italian cuisine.

Our customers love the daily specials! Many of our aficionados don't even bother with the main menu any more. This is a great vote of confidence for us, as it reflects a mutual trust which has developed over time.

Importantly, constant development of the daily special has allowed us to keep in close contact with the best and most original expression of this culinary aspect of Italian culture. At home we often joke that not having the opportunity to continuously explore (and therefore keep close to) Italian food would be akin to not allowing our relations in Donegal to enjoy a good cup of tea.

Being presented with all those flavours first thing in the morning is akin to a daily journey back to a sense of intimate familiarity, where tastes and smells bring back memories; images of the ordinary and mundane which are now a reminder of a nostalgic sense of the past, a fantasy which can only exist in our own memory.

Our local open-air market in Rome is magically recreated every morning at the back of the restaurant, with deliveries of fresh vegetables, organic meats, eggs, fish and breads. The only thing missing is the interesting people one meets at these markets, always ready, nay eager, to suggest a recipe or an improvement on a recipe. And without knowing it we have taken on that role of suggesting recipes and dishes.

We find ourselves always reminding our younger chefs of the importance of respecting traditional recipes, as a good understanding of these will give a chef the bones, the structure, the key. They form the *Bunreacht na hÉireann* of Italian cooking.

As with most things, it is important to have strong points of reference. We believe that to change traditional recipes to suit a particular taste or sell more dishes, as is so prevalent in the sector, is extremely damaging to these culinary milestones. It is what we consider the end of good cooking.

essere in costante contatto con la miglior parte, la più genuina espressione di un aspetto della cultura italiana. Per noi vivere senza cibo italiano sarebbe forse la condanna più mostruosa che si possa ricevere, come togliere del tè ad una Signora Irlandese.

Ripassare i sapori al mattino è come riambientarsi in qualcosa a te familiare i cui sapori e odori ti riportano a ricordi ed impressioni dove ti appaiono immagini a te familiari; forse non apprezzate quando eri in Italia perché li a portata di mano, ma di cui senti la mancanza appena te ne scosti.

Il ricevere ogni giorno verdure, carne, uova, pane, pesce e crostacei pensare come trasformarli o come ricavarne del gusto ti sembra come se nel retro negozio quasi d'incanto avessi ricreato un mercato all'aperto. Come quei mercati di cui ogni città italiana ne è piena in ogni area e quartiere e dove incontri il tuo verduriere, o macellaio o pescivendolo di fiducia che ti suggeriscono, prodotti sempre nuovi interessanti e via via senza dartene l'impressione ti suggeriscono ricette o modi di come conservarli. Rivedere quei prodotti la mattina è come rivivere tutte quelle emozioni e senza accorgersene esser passato dall'altra parte ritrovandosi a suggerir ricette.

Ed è importante, quello che dico sempre ai cuochi e cerco di spiegare ai clienti, le ricette originali vanno sempre rispettate perché danno l'ossatura, la struttura, sono la Carta Costituzionale di una cucina.

Cambiare, imbastardire le ricette pensando di adattarle a questo o quel gusto o per venderne di più, come fanno nell'idustria, non serve, anzi, è estremamente dannoso perché non si hanno più punti di riferimento culinari. E questo è la fine della buona cucina.

Inventarne di nuove si, è lì l'abilità e la differenza tra chi è riuscito ad assimilare la cucina italiana come fattore culturale e chi no, tra chi si può dire che cucini italiano e chi no. È questo che rende la cucina italiana anchora viva.

The skill is in creating new, clearly identifiable Italian dishes. This is what sets apart those who have been able to understand and assimilate Italian cooking from a cultural perspective, and those who have not. It is the difference between those who merit the distinction of being called a chef of Italian cuisine and those who do not.

There is no tradition of restaurateurs in either mine or Eileen's family. However, there is a strong culinary tradition. Our approach to restaurant cooking has by extension derived from this smaller family context, scaled up to cater for many more people.

For several years now we have been importing produce from Italy. It all started about fifteen years ago, when we started importing regional wines from small Italian wineries. Our aim was simply to share and raise an awareness amongst our customers of the multitudes of wines which we had the pleasure of enjoying over the years in Italy. Today we import close to 200 different wines, trying to represent a fair geographical spread of the entire peninsula. The wine producers we choose tend to be small, family-run businesses or co-operatives, where profit and the commercialisation of the industry is not the first objective and where quality is guaranteed by containing the scale of production.

I am not a great believer in lengthy introductions. More often than not I find them boring and distracting from the principal message the book aims to put across. They are frequently a post-rationalisation of the many ideas which have been involuntarily penned through a less conscious and freer process. So to conclude, one thing became apparent as we journeyed through the writing of this book: we did not know that we had much to say on the matter. But now that we have started we have realised that perhaps one book may not be sufficient …

Kind regards,

Stefano Crescenzi

Nella mia famiglia non c' una tradizione di ristoratori ma sicuramente una tradizione culinaria e cucinare per pochi o per molti alla fine non fa molta differenza.

Da un paio di anni abbiamo intrapreso a parallelo della ristorazione anche l'importazione di prodotti alimentarí dall'Italia. Abbiamo iniziato più di quindici anni fa con il vino semplicemente perché volevamo importare del vino che ci piacesse di più e farlo conoscere ai nostri clienti, oggi importiamo circa 200 etichette diverse distribuite un po' per tutta l'Italia soprattutto da piccoli produttori o cooperative, dove il profitto non è per statuto il primo obiettivo aziendale e dove si salvaguardia maggiormente la piccola produzione e la qualità. Ora importiamo anche molti prodotti della terra e il 'mercato quasi virtuale quello del "retro megozio"' di cui parlavo prima si è allargato, e allargato e lo trovo particolarmente attraente anche perchè ci permette di rendere vivo il rapporto con l'Italia attraverso visite in loco o fiere alimentari, ci tiene in continuo dialogo con la produzione e la cucina italiana. Tutto ciò è divenuto na sorta di continua formazione professionale tanto che a volte siamo più informati noi che gli italiani stessi.

Non ho mai creduto alle lunghe introduzioni, anzi ho sempre pensato che sono noiose e ti distraggono dal testo principale, dall'obiettivo del libro stesso.Come se uno dovesse per forza spiegare razionalmente quello che la penna involontariamente ha trasmesso.

Non mi voglio dilungare, quindi, oltre misura ma una cosa è certa che quando abbiamo iniziato a scrivere non sapevamo di aver tante cose da raccontarvi, e ora che abbiamo iniziato abbiamo scoperto che un libro non basta e che ce ne vorranno degli altri.

Cordiali Saluti,

Stefano Crescenzi

Sourcing our ingredients

At Dunne & Crescenzi we pride ourselves on sourcing the perfect combination of fresh Irish produce and specially imported authentic Italian products. When we returned to Ireland from Italy in 1995, it was next to impossible to get good olive oils, balsamic vinegar, parmesan and other cheeses in Ireland. And so 'La Vista', our original deli on Strand Road in Sutton, was born. We started to import large drums of olive oils (our customers would bring their own bottles to fill up!), as well as cheeses, vinegar, pesto, coffee and salumi.

However, in the last few years there has been an explosion of artisan food production in Ireland and we find we don't have to rely as much on imports from Italy.

We are forever grateful to our partners in Ireland who provide us with the best of Irish local food. McConnells of Dublin's smoked Irish salmon is probably the best I have ever had. Gold River organic farm in Wicklow delivers seasonal vegetables, jams and honey from G's Gourmet Jams of County Laois go into our tarts, Kerry Lamb Group provide us with excellent lamb, and the historic Downey's butcher of Terenure in Dublin supplies the rest of our meat and game.

Some key ingredients such as good extra virgin olive oils, wines, particular cheeses and salumi still need to be shipped over to stock our *Dispensa* or pantry. Salcis of Siena sends us wonderful fresh sheep ricotta, pecorino cheese and speciality sausages, Villani of Emilia Romagna sends us Prosciutto di Parma and a variety of salumi, and Consorzio Grana Trentino dispatches huge wheels of grana cheese. How and why a particular supplier is chosen often depends on a chance meeting or a nostalgic event, and it's great when our partners share the same beliefs regarding respect for the environment and sustainability. It is important to build a relationship with suppliers and I always enjoy our weekly chats about availability and what to expect in the coming weeks, as well as sharing recipes with them.

DUNNE &
CRESCENZI

D&C

cafe/deli

CRESCENZI

DUNNE & CRESCENZI

Castelgreve

DUNNE & CRESCENZI

CASTELLI del GREVEPESA

CHIANTI CLASSICO

Antipasti

Dunne & Crescenzi, at South Frederick Street, started life as a very small wine bar with a range of antipasti. Since then, the menu has extended to include *primi* (pasta and risotto dishes) and *secondi* (main courses). Nonetheless antipasti continue to be very popular with customers. *Pasto* is a meal and *antipasto* (singular of antipasti) refers to something eaten before the meal, a starter.

Most traditional restaurants in Italy are equipped with long fridges offering wonderful arrays of antipasti. These largely consist of cold dishes such as selections of local salumi (*charcuterie*) such as salami, prosciutto, speck, mortadella and bresaola, and grilled and marinated seasonal vegetables. Along the coastal areas squid salad or warm dishes of *zuppa di cozze* (sauté of mussels) would be common. Nowadays Italians living in the major cities no longer have time for long leisurely lunches, so plates of antipasti offer a good alternative. However, antipasti are still very prevalent as starter options for lingering evening diners. Large serving plates are placed in the middle of the table and everyone helps themselves.

Making antipasti broadly consists of assembling food; the better the quality of produce, the nicer the *antipasto* will be. The dressing is also very important and it can make or break a dish. Cheap olive oil will leave a nasty tang on your antipasti whereas a quality olive oil will enhance the dish. We use extra virgin olive oil from Puglia with distinctive nutty notes and high in polyphenols in the kitchen, and oils from Lazio, Tuscany, Umbria and Puglia for dressings. There is nothing quite as nice as nibbling on a chunk of country loaf dipped in good olive oil!

Artisan production of local food is prevalent in Italian local cuisines; wonderful cured meats, crafted cheeses, preserved fruits and vegetables, and baked breads are part of everyday life. Ancient skills and techniques, which originated because of the necessity to preserve food, are still used in the modern society. These skills and products, which were largely associated with the *cucina povera* (peasant cuisine), have now evolved into elaborate businesses committed to the protocol of 'Protected Designation of Origin' foods, wines and oils. These wonderful foods are widely available in the fruit and vegetable *mercati* (markets). Every town and village hosts their daily *mercato*, and *mercati* are to be found dotted around the cities.

Farmers markets, which mirror the *mercati* of our Mediterranean neighbours, are mushrooming around Ireland, providing a welcome outlet for artisan produce in Ireland.

GRILLED MEDITERRANEAN VEGETABLES

Delizie dell'orto

Vegetables are best grilled on a barbecue, but you can use a griddle pan at home.

INGREDIENTS – SERVES 4

2 medium aubergines
2 medium peppers, one yellow and
    one red bell
2 medium courgettes
12 button mushrooms
Salt

Dressing
150ml extra virgin olive oil
2 cloves of garlic, crushed
2 tablespoons of flat-leaf parsley,
    finely chopped
1 tablespoon of balsamic vinegar
Salt and ground black pepper

METHOD

- With a pestle and mortar pound all of the dry ingredients for the dressing, then add the oil and vinegar and leave to rest.

- Slice the aubergines thinly (1cm) and spread the slices on a large tray. Sprinkle with salt and leave for 30 minutes. Then rinse off the salt under cold running water and pat dry the aubergines. Slice the courgettes lengthways as thinly as possible. Remove the stems from the mushrooms (these can be used for soups).

- On a very hot griddle pan sear the aubergines, mushrooms and courgettes, one batch at a time. Turn them over several times – this should take about five minutes. Remove to a serving dish, drizzle with the dressing and leave to cool. Sear the peppers on a very hot griddle pan, turning them over regularly until they blacken and blister. This can take 10 to 15 minutes. Remove, run under the cold tap briefly and peel off the black skin. (Alternatively you can roast the peppers in the oven for about 40 minutes.)

- Slice open the peppers, remove the pulp and seeds, and cut into 4cm strips. Dress and leave to rest.

- Arrange the vegetables on a large platter and serve with crusty bread or *bruschetta semplice* (bread toasted on both sides, then rubbed lightly with garlic and drizzled with extra virgin olive oil).

  Suggestion: It is worth doing double the amount and keeping some in the fridge for a couple of days.

CAMPANIA BUFFALO MOZZARELLA, AUBERGINE AND PRAWN STACK

Millefoglie di bufala di Campania con gamberi, melanzane e pesto

Buffalo mozzarella is made from buffalo milk (*mozzarella vaccina* is made from cow's milk). The herds are prominent in the Campania region, the area around Naples. You can drop into one of the many *caseifici* (artisan cheese makers) along the Naples to Rome route and enjoy freshly made mozzarella. The owners are generally happy to make up panini of thick slices of *pagnotta* (wood oven-baked bread), ripe plum tomatoes and warm mozzarella drizzled with local olive oil. Sit on the plastic chairs outside, ignore the traffic and indulge in one of life's simple pleasures.

INGREDIENTS – SERVES 4

  4 thick slices of fresh buffalo mozzarella
  4 slices of grilled aubergine *(see recipe on page 27)*
  4 fresh king prawns, cleaned and shelled
  4 tablespoons of extra virgin olive oil
  4 tablespoons of fresh Genovese pesto *(see recipe on page 55)*

METHOD

- Seal the prawns in a little hot olive oil, just a minute on each side.
- Stack the ingredients by placing a slice of aubergine on top of the mozzarella and sit a prawn on top.
- Dress with extra virgin olive oil and serve with a dollop of fresh pesto on the side and toasted ciabatta or breadsticks.

Suggestion: Buffalo mozzarella should never be served cold straight from the fridge. Immerse the mozzarella in warm water for 30 seconds just before cutting and eating.

BRESAOLA FROM VALTELLINA, ROCKET AND PARMIGIANO

Bresaola di Valtellina, rughetta e parmigiano

Bresaola is a speciality beef from Valtellina in Lombardy, cured with herbs and spices. It is very lean, a noble ingredient for antipasti and salads.

INGREDIENTS – SERVES 4

24 wafer-thin slices of bresaola
100g fresh rocket
200g parmigiano shavings
16 tablespoons of extra virgin olive oil
Juice of 2 lemons, freshly squeezed

METHOD

- Mix the oil and lemon juice together.
- Lay the bresaola slices on a large serving dish and cover with the rocket and parmigiano shavings.
- Drizzle with plenty of the oil and lemon juice mixture.

Suggestion: Bresaola is high in iron, a good source of energy if you are feeling under the weather.

PORTOBELLO MUSHROOMS WITH GORGONZOLA AND PESTO STUFFING

Funghi ripieni di Gorgonzola e pesto

Alberto, Ligurian to the core and executive chef of our restaurant *Nonna Valentina*, introduced this antipasto to the restaurant. You can also enjoy this in one of the little trattorie near St Paul's Cathedral, Portovenere, on the breathtaking Ligurian coast.

INGREDIENTS – SERVES 4

4 Portobello mushrooms, cleaned
250g Gorgonzola cheese, crumbled
200g breadcrumbs
4 heaped tablespoons of Genovese pesto *(see recipe on page 55)*
2 tablespoons of extra virgin olive oil

METHOD

- Preheat the oven to 180 degrees.
- Remove the stalks from the mushrooms.
- Mix the breadcrumbs and pesto together to form a paste and fold in half of the crumbled Gorgonzola.
- Lightly brush the mushroom caps with the oil and place upside down on a baking tin.
- Fill the mushrooms with the Gorgonzola and pesto stuffing, top with the rest of the Gorgonzola and bake for around 15 minutes.

Suggestion: The pesto stuffing is quite filling so these are best served on their own.

SMOKED IRISH SALMON WITH AVOCADO, GOAT'S CHEESE AND ROCKET

Rotolini di salmone irlandese affumicato con avocado, caprino e rughetta

La Vigilia di Natale/Christmas Eve is celebrated throughout Italy with a fish dinner, and smoked Irish salmon, which is considered a luxury food, is given a place of honour amongst the starters.

INGREDIENTS – SERVES 4

16 slices of smoked Irish salmon or 120g per person
2 mature avocados, peeled and diced
200g fresh goat's cheese
100g rocket (or rucola)
Juice of 2 lemons
8 tablespoons of extra virgin olive oil
Freshly ground black pepper

METHOD

- Lay the salmon slices on a large serving platter and dot with the avocado and crumbled goat's cheese and finish off with the rocket/rucola. Drizzle with the oil and lemon juice, and add some freshly ground black pepper.
- Serve with fresh or toasted brown bread. We also prepare this dish with grapefruit instead of goat's cheese and garnish with chives.

Suggestion: The success of this dish is dependent on a really good smoked salmon and mature avocados. Here in Ireland we have fantastic smoked salmon: source it from a small producer.

CAMPANIA BUFFALO MOZZARELLA WITH GRILLED PEPPERS AND FRESH BASIL

Mozzarella di bufala di Campania con peperoni grigliati e basilico

A good buffalo mozzarella should be firm, squeak when it is cut and be creamy on the palate.

INGREDIENTS – SERVES 4

4 fresh buffalo mozzarella balls of 150g each
4 grilled peppers *(see recipe on page 27)*
4 tablespoons of extra virgin olive oil
Bunch of fresh basil
Salt to taste

METHOD

- Mix the peppers and basil together along with a tablespoon of the oil.

- Cut each mozzarella ball into three slices.

- Alternate a slice of mozzarella with a tablespoon of peppers and spread out on a large serving platter, until all of the ingredients are used.

- Drizzle with oil and salt to taste. Serve on a bed of rocket with toasted bread or breadsticks.

Suggestion: We prefer buffalo mozzarella from the Campania region in our salads and antipasti, and cow's mozzarella (vaccina) for cooked dishes.

PROSCIUTTO SAN DANIELE WITH BABY SPINACH, GRANA TRENTINO CHEESE SHAVINGS AND RADICCHIO

Prosciutto San Daniele con insalatina di spinaci, scaglie di Grana Trentino e radicchio

This dish incorporates all five tastes – sweet (prosciutto and honey), sour (lemon), bitter (radicchio and spinach), salty (prosciutto) and savoury/umani (Grana).

INGREDIENTS – SERVES 4

8 wafer-thin slices of Prosciutto San Daniele
200g baby spinach, washed
4 large radicchio leaves, washed
200g Grana Trentino cheese flakes
4 tablespoons of extra virgin olive oil
25g honey
Juice of 2 lemons

METHOD

- Toss the baby spinach leaves with the oil and lemon juice.
- Divide the radicchio leaves between 4 plates.
- Fill the leaves with spinach and top with slices of Prosciutto San Daniele (2 per dish), sprinkle with Grana Trentino cheese flakes and serve with honey on the side.

Suggestion: You can use Gorgonzola or soft goat's cheese instead of Grana Trentino.

SAUTÉ OF MUSSELS

Sauté di cozze

I love the sound of empty mussels being discarded by diners on a side plate, an echo of satisfaction that breaks through the din of a busy restaurant.

INGREDIENTS – SERVES 4

2kg mussels
3 cloves of garlic, peeled
12 cherry tomatoes, halved
6 tablespoons of extra virgin olive oil
1 teaspoon of dried chilli flakes
½ glass of dry white wine
½ glass of warm water
Bunch of flat-leaf parsley, chopped

METHOD

- Discard any broken or open mussels, then scrub and remove the beards from the rest.
- Steep in plenty of cold water for at least 1 hour and change the water several times.
- Sauté the garlic and chilli in the oil on a low heat but do not let the garlic brown.
- Add the tomatoes and cook for 2 minutes, then add the mussels and wine. Increase the heat momentarily to cook off the alcohol, then return to a low heat.
- Pour in the water, cover and cook until the mussels have opened; discard any unopened mussels.
- Serve with parsley and plenty of toasted country loaf drizzled with extra virgin olive oil.

Suggestion: You can cook paccheri pasta and serve this with the mussels and sauce instead of bread. If the mussels are open before cooking try tapping them on the side of a bowl and they might close – if not, discard.

SPECK AND ASIAGO POLENTA CROSTINI
Crostini di polenta con speck e Asiago

Smokey speck (a smoked variant of prosciutto from the Alpine regions) enhances and gives depth to the polenta and Asiago, both mild in flavour.

INGREDIENTS – SERVES 4

320g polenta, cooked *(see recipe on page 194)*
8 slices of speck
8 thick slices of Asiago cheese
4 tablespoons of extra virgin olive oil
2 tablespoons of balsamic vinegar

METHOD

- Prepare the polenta, leave to cool and cut into 8 rectangles.
- Place the rectangles on a hot grill and turn over a couple of times until warmed through.
- Place the polenta on a warm serving dish and set a thick slice of Asiago cheese on top, then wrap in speck.
- Drizzle with the oil and balsamic vinegar, and serve immediately.

Suggestion: After you have warmed through the polenta you might like to place the Asiago cheese on top and place under a grill until it melts and then wrap with speck.

POLENTA AND SPINACH CROSTINI
Crostini di polenta con spinaci

- Prepare the polenta crostini as above without the speck and top with garlic and chilli spinach *(see recipe on page 204)*.

BRUSCHETTA WITH FRESH VINE-RIPENED TOMATOES AND BASIL

Bruschetta con pomodoro e basilico

Bruschetta, from the word *bruscare*, to roast or toast, is probably the most popular and widely diffused antipasto in Italy. The simplest version consists of toasting bread on both sides then rubbing lightly with garlic and drizzling with extra virgin olive oil – we call this *bruschetta semplice*. There is a whole section on our menu dedicated to *bruschetteria* and, while the combinations are many, our favourite remains *bruschetta al pomodoro*, with fresh ripe tomatoes, good extra virgin olive oil and fresh basil.

INGREDIENTS – SERVES 4

4 thick slices of country loaf
4 vine-ripened beef tomatoes, chopped
8 leaves of fresh basil, shredded
4 tablespoons of extra virgin olive oil
1 clove of garlic, peeled
Salt to taste

METHOD

- Toss the tomatoes, basil, salt and oil in a bowl and leave to rest for 5 minutes.
- Toast the bread and then rub the warm bread with garlic and spoon the tomatoes and juice on top. Serve immediately.

Suggestion: We do not recommend that you rub the bread with garlic or drizzle with oil prior to toasting; do this when the bread is hot and nicely toasted.

BRUSCHETTA WITH MUSHROOMS AND RICOTTA BOWS

Bruschetta con funghi misti e fiocchi di ricotta

Salcis in Siena send us fresh sheep ricotta every week, and the sight of those pearly white baskets of fresh ricotta sends waves of delightful emotion throughout the restaurant.

INGREDIENTS – SERVES 4

4 thick slices of country loaf or ciabatta bread
300g champignon mushrooms, cleaned and finely chopped
200g fresh ricotta
4 tablespoons of extra virgin olive oil
1 tablespoon of flat-leaf parsley, chopped
1 shallot, finely sliced
1 clove of garlic, peeled
Salt and freshly ground black pepper to taste

METHOD

- Sweat the shallot in the oil on a low heat until it becomes translucent and add the mushrooms.
- Cover and continue to cook for 5 minutes, then add the parsley, salt and pepper.
- Meanwhile toast the bread on both sides in a toaster or under the grill.
- Rub each warm slice with the garlic, top with the mushroom mixture and delicately dot with the ricotta. Serve immediately as this is best eaten warm.

Suggestion: Various varieties of mushrooms are readily available – feel free to use any of them.

BRUSCHETTA WITH TUNA, OLIVES, CAPERS AND SUN-DRIED TOMATOES

Bruschetta con tonno, olive, capperi e pomodori secchi

Tuna, olives, capers and sun-dried tomatoes, a homage to a summer's day in Palermo!

INGREDIENTS – SERVES 4

4 thick slices of country loaf
250g tuna preserved in olive oil
50g sun-dried tomatoes, shredded
16 taggiasche olives
1 tablespoon of salted capers, rinsed and dried
1 clove of garlic, peeled
4 tablespoons of extra virgin olive oil
Juice of 1 lemon

METHOD

- Toss the tuna, capers, olives and sun-dried tomatoes in a bowl with the oil and lemon juice and leave to rest for 5 minutes.
- Toast the bread on both sides and then rub lightly with garlic.
- Spread the mixture thickly on top and serve while the bread is still hot.

Suggestion: You can blitz tuna, sun-dried tomatoes, oil and lemon juice together in a blender to obtain a coarse paste, then spread it on the bruschetta and top with olives and capers.

BAKED CROSTINI WITH ANCHOVIES, PROSCIUTTO DI PARMA, PARMIGIANO AND ROCKET

Crostini caldi dal forno

Crostini are another form of bruschetta and make for delicious appetisers, ideally served with prosecco. Bake trays of crostini to cater for large get-togethers of family and friends.

INGREDIENTS – SERVES 4–6

12 slices of ciabatta loaf (2cm thick)
12 thick slices of fresh mozzarella
12 salted anchovies
6 wafer-thin slices of Prosciutto di Parma
2 ripe beef tomatoes, diced
100g parmigiano shavings
50g rocket
8 tablespoons of extra virgin olive oil (for anchovy dressing)
4 tablespoons of extra virgin olive oil (dressing for prosciutto crostini)
2 teaspoons of white wine vinegar

METHOD

- Preheat the oven to 180 degrees. Take a pestle and mortar and pound the anchovies, oil and vinegar to form an anchovy paste.

- Place a slice of mozzarella on each piece of bread. Spread a little anchovy paste on 6 of the slices of mozzarella.

- Bake the entire batch on a lightly oiled oven tray for 10 minutes in a hot oven until the mozzarella melts.

- Place thin slices of Prosciutto di Parma on the six crostini without anchovy paste and return to the oven for 1 minute, then smother in fresh rocket and parmigiano shavings, dot with tomato and serve immediately drizzled with extra virgin olive oil.

Suggestion: For vegetarian crostini spread some sun-dried tomato pesto on slices of ciabatta bread, top with mozzarella and bake.

BRUSCHETTA WITH BORLOTTI BEANS AND TOMATO

Bruschetta con fagioli e salsa di pomodoro

Beans cooked in tomato sauce are probably the precursor of commercial baked beans. This traditional recipe is both rustic and elegant and as such calls for a good full-bodied wine to accompany it.

INGREDIENTS – SERVES 4

200g cooked borlotti or cannellini beans *(see recipe on page 209)* (rinse and drain canned beans before using)
150ml tomato passata
1 shallot, finely sliced
1 clove of garlic, peeled
4 tablespoons of extra virgin olive oil
2 tablespoons of balsamic vinegar
4 thick slices of rustic country bread
Salt and freshly ground black pepper

METHOD

- Sweat the shallot in the oil and add the beans, then add the vinegar followed by the tomato.

- Cook on a low heat for 10 minutes, then add salt and plenty of freshly ground black pepper to taste.

- Toast 4 slices of bread on both sides and while hot rub gently with the garlic. Spoon over the beans with a dash of sauce and plenty of black pepper, and serve immediately.

Suggestion: Do not put too much sauce on the bruschetta or it will become soggy.

Pesto

Pesto comes from the verb *pestare*, meaning to pound, and the ingredients are pounded with a pestle in a mortar. Pesto can be made with most vegetables and nuts – the list is endless. We serve olive, sun-dried tomato, Genovese, artichoke and hazelnut pesto. These are served on crostini or used to dress pasta. To create crostini with pesto, toast some thick slices of country loaf or ciabatta bread on both sides and spread with pesto while the bread is still warm. It is best not to rub the bread with garlic as it will interfere with the flavours of the pesto.

BLACK OLIVE PESTO
Pesto di olive

INGREDIENTS
200g pitted Gaeta olives
4 tablespoons of extra virgin olive oil
Bunch of flat-leaf parsley
1 clove of garlic, peeled
Freshly ground black pepper to taste

METHOD
- Blitz all of the ingredients in a blender until you obtain a creamy consistency; add a little more oil if it becomes too thick.

Suggestion: Spread on warm crostini as an appetiser or spread over fish fillets like sea bass, cod or haddock and roast in the oven.

SUN-DRIED TOMATO PESTO
Pesto di pomodori secchi

INGREDIENTS
200g sun-dried tomatoes
6 tablespoons of extra virgin olive oil
1 clove of garlic, peeled
2 salted anchovies (optional)
¼ teaspoon of fresh lemon zest
¼ teaspoon of dried chilli flakes

METHOD
- Blitz all of the ingredients in a blender until you obtain a creamy consistency; add a little more oil if it becomes too thick.

Suggestion: Spread on warm crostini or panini with some goat's cheese.

ALBERTO'S GENOVESE BASIL PESTO
Pesto Genovese

INGREDIENTS
100g fresh basil leaves
100g freshly grated parmigiano
50g Mediterranean pine nuts*
30g peeled almonds
2 cloves of crushed garlic
150ml extra virgin olive oil

METHOD
- Blitz all of the dry ingredients in a blender with half of the oil, then add the rest of the oil and blitz again until you obtain a creamy consistency.

Suggestion: Use as a sauce for pasta. For example see the recipe for tonnarelli with potato and string beans on page 115. Basil pesto marries well with all mozzarella-based antipasti.

HAZELNUT PESTO
Pesto di nocciole

INGREDIENTS
150g crushed hazelnuts
150ml extra virgin olive oil
50g grated parmigiano
Bunch of flat-leaf parsley

METHOD
- Blitz the hazelnuts in a blender and then add the oil, parmigiano and parsley, and blitz again to obtain a creamy consistency.

Suggestion: Use as a sauce for pasta and gnocchi mixed with a little fresh cream.

ARTICHOKE PESTO
Pesto di carciofi

INGREDIENTS
4 artichoke hearts, cleaned *(see recipe on page 201)* and ready for cooking, or a jar of artichokes, rinsed and drained
2 cloves of garlic, crushed
150ml extra virgin olive oil
¼ teaspoon of lemon zest
Bunch of flat-leaf parsley

METHOD
- If you are using fresh artichokes simmer them in a saucepan of salted water, along with half a lemon, for about 30 minutes until soft. Blitz all of the ingredients (using fresh or preserved artichokes) in a blender until you have obtained a creamy consistency; add a little more oil if it becomes too thick.

* There is a condition called pine mouth and the World Health Organisation has been following up on reports from consumers who suffer from a loss of taste for several weeks having consumed pine nuts from other continents. Just to be safe you might want to purchase Mediterranean pine nuts.

Soups

Le Zuppe

Back in 1975 when I first arrived in Italy the most popular soups were *brodo* (broth), clear vegetable or meat broths with ditalini pasta sprinkled with parmigiano, *tortellini in brodo*, clear vegetable broth with prosciutto-filled tortellini pasta, or *stracciatella*, a clear meat or vegetable broth with whisked egg. Substantial soups like *zuppa di fagioli* (bean soup) or *zuppa di ceci* (chickpea soup) are more akin to pasta dishes. Nowadays, *vellutate*, velvety or creamy soups such as pea or pumpkin, can be found on the menus of famous and aspiring chefs, influenced by foreign cuisines. *Minestra* covers a multitude of soups, usually homemade. Unlike other pasta or main courses where large platters are placed in the centre of the table and everyone helps themselves, *minestra* soup is served *amministrato*, ladled into soup bowls. *Minestrone*, a thick vegetable soup, features on our menu throughout the year by popular demand.

MINESTRONE SOUP

Minestrone

Minestrone soup should change depending what vegetable is in season – a little cabbage or spinach, a couple of courgettes, fresh peas or broad beans. This is our basic recipe at the restaurant.

INGREDIENTS – SERVES 4

200g dried ditalini pasta from
    Gragnano
2 carrots, diced
2 onions, diced
2 celery sticks, diced
2 courgettes, diced
2 ripe beef tomatoes, chopped
1 medium potato, diced

150g string beans, cut in half
150g cooked borlotti beans *(see recipe on page 209)* or tinned borlotti beans, rinsed and drained
50g freshly grated parmigiano
6 tablespoons of olive oil
Salt and pepper to taste

METHOD

- Sauté the onions, carrots and celery in the oil over a gentle heat for about 5 minutes, add the string beans and tomatoes and stir.
- Cover the vegetables with cold water, add salt, bring to the boil and simmer for 15 minutes.
- Now add the potato and courgettes and continue to simmer for 10 minutes.
- Add the borlotti beans and continue to cook for an additional 5 minutes.
- Meanwhile cook the ditalini pasta according to the instructions on the packet, drain and add to the soup just before serving.
- Serve with freshly grated parmigiano and ground black pepper.

Suggestion: Swirl a spoonful of Genovese pesto into the minestrone for an interesting visual effect and taste. In Italy, the rind of parmigiano is scrubbed and cooked in this soup. It adds a lovely sweetness to the soup and the softened squidgy cheese is wonderful to chew on.

BORLOTTI BEAN SOUP
Zuppa di fagioli

Zuppa di fagioli is the epitome of comfort food, and just as every region has a recipe for making salami the same applies to bean soup. In Milan they make a cream of borlotti; further south lard(o) is fried with the soffritto.* This is our favourite recipe.

INGREDIENTS – SERVES 6

200g dried borlotti beans
200g ditalini pasta
100g freshly grated parmigiano
6 tablespoons of extra virgin olive oil
2 cloves of garlic, peeled
1 level teaspoon of dried chilli flakes
½ glass of red wine
1 ripe beef tomato, chopped
Freshly ground black pepper

METHOD

- Cook the borlotti beans *(see recipe on page 209)*, then drain the beans, but retain the cooking broth.

- Bring the broth to boiling point and cook the pasta in it. Blitz half of the beans in a blender along with a couple of tablespoons of broth.

- In a large heavy-based saucepan sauté the garlic and chilli in the oil and add the tomato.

- Then stir in the blended beans, pour in the wine and increase the heat momentarily to cook off the alcohol, then return to a low heat.

- Once the pasta is cooked *al dente*, add the contents of the saucepan to the pot of pasta and stir.

- Fold in the rest of the beans and serve with plenty of parmigiano and freshly ground black pepper.

*Soffritto is the basis of a lot of Italian dishes and consists of finely diced carrot, celery and onion or shallot which is gently fried in olive oil.

BUTTERNUT SQUASH, SCALLOP AND ALMOND SOUP

Crema di zucca, mandorle e capesante

This festive soup appears on the menu around Halloween, a prelude to Christmas.

INGREDIENTS – SERVES 4

800g butternut squash, cleaned and diced
500ml vegetable broth *(see recipe on page 133)*
8 scallops (remove the corals)
1 medium potato, diced
2 shallots, finely sliced
2 tablespoons of almond shavings
4 tablespoons of extra virgin olive oil
Salt and pepper to taste
Sprig of thyme

METHOD

- Place the butternut squash on a baking tray and cook in a hot oven for 15 minutes or until soft.

- Lightly pan toast the almonds for a minute on a hot skillet and set aside.

- Sweat the shallots in the oil over a low heat until they become translucent, then add the butternut squash, potato, thyme, salt and pepper along with the vegetable broth.

- Cover and simmer for 10 minutes. Remove from the heat, take out the thyme and blend the rest with a hand mixer to obtain a creamy consistency, then return to the heat.

- Meanwhile sear the scallops on both sides in a pan with a little extra oil for 2 minutes.

- Ladle the soup into 4 bowls, place 2 scallops into each serving and sprinkle with the toasted almonds.

CHICKPEA SOUP WITH PASTA

Zuppa di ceci

When Italians talk about the best *pasta all'amatriciana* they have ever tasted, they are not only talking about the quality of the dish but also about who made it (nonna/grandmother), where (in the house/in the village), who was there (at least twenty-five relatives and friends!), when (every Easter) and with what (Zio Alberto's guanciale (cured pork cheek) and Zia Maria's *pomodoro*). It's the recalling of the entire event that makes it so good. Strong family bonds are reinforced through associations with food. A well-known Italian chef, Gualtiero Marchesi, founder of the Alma cookery school, once said, 'I fear that the younger generations will not remember their grandmothers' cooking.' I don't think Gualtiero Marchesi need worry yet. We work with a large number of young Italian waiters and chefs in the restaurant and they are just as eager as their grandmothers to discuss recipes; they get excited about a good *zuppa di ceci* and their social lives seem to consist mainly of organising *cene* (dinners).

INGREDIENTS – SERVES 6

200g spaghetti
200g chickpeas
100g freshly grated parmigiano
2 cloves of garlic, peeled
½ teaspoon of dried chilli flakes
½ glass of dry white wine
Sprig of rosemary

METHOD

- Cook the chickpeas *(see recipe on page 209)* then blitz half of them in a blender with a couple of spoons of the cooking broth. Return the saucepan with the rest of the chickpeas and broth to the heat and bring to boiling point.

- Break the spaghetti into small pieces and cook in the broth for 10 minutes or so.

- Meanwhile sauté the garlic, rosemary and chilli in a pan, remove the rosemary with a slotted spoon and stir in the blended chickpeas from the blender.

- Heat through, pour in the wine and increase the heat momentarily to cook off the alcohol, then return to a low heat.
- Add this to the saucepan with the chickpeas, broth and spaghetti. Serve when the pasta is cooked and sprinkle with the freshly grated parmigiano.

Suggestion: I love to make this dish with rigatoni, much to Stefano's amusement – he prefers small pasta for soupy dishes while I get more satisfaction from the bite of a larger pasta.

LENTIL AND MUSSEL SOUP

Zuppa di lenticchie e cozze

Inspired by our trips to the Marche, this soup combines Castelluccio lentils from the Sibelline hills and mussels from Porto San Giorgio on the coast.

INGREDIENTS – SERVES 4

400g cooked chilli and garlic lentils *(see recipe on page 210)*
200g cooked mussels *(see recipe on page 41)*
150ml vegetable broth *(see recipe on page 133)*
Bunch of flat-leaf parsley, finely chopped

METHOD

- Remove the mussels from their shells.
- Simmer the chilli and garlic lentils in a saucepan with the vegetable broth and warm through, fold in the mussels and serve with the parsley and *bruschetta semplice (see page 45)*.

Suggestion: For a vellutata of lentils you can blend the lentils, warm through and fold in the mussels. Colfiorito lentils from Umbria are also very good but harder to find outside of Italy.

PEA, PRAWN AND MINT SOUP
Vellutata di piselli e menta con gamberi

The most memorable soup I ever tasted was at Gennaro Esposito's restaurant *Torre di Saracino* in Vico Equense on the Bay of Naples.

INGREDIENTS – SERVES 4

400g fresh or frozen peas
500ml vegetable broth *(see recipe on page 133)*
2 shallots, finely sliced
1 medium potato, diced
4 fresh mint leaves
8 fresh Dublin Bay prawns, cleaned and shelled
4 tablespoons of extra virgin olive oil
Salt and pepper to taste

METHOD

- Cook the peas in simmering broth for 5 minutes.

- Meanwhile sweat the shallots in a wide pot in the oil on a low heat until they become translucent.

- Add the potato and mint and stir, then add the peas along with the cooking broth, a little salt and pepper (remember that the broth is salty, so don't add too much extra salt). Cover and simmer for 10 minutes.

- Blend the soup with a hand mixer and return to the heat. Sear the prawns on both sides in a little extra oil for 2 minutes. Ladle the soup into 4 dishes and place 2 prawns into each serving.

Suggestion: Prepare the pea soup as above but use 2 medium potatoes instead of one and you will obtain a thicker consistency. Serve this pea cream with fish or stuffed calamari.

Salads

Insalate

Salads are eaten daily in Italy almost as a staple food and you may be surprised when you visit Italy that your salad will consist of a mere handful of cos leaves and a couple of slices of tomato, dressed with olive oil and white wine vinegar, but the tomatoes will be delicious. In fact while dining in Furore recently I ended up ordering four plates of tomatoes – they were so good and the oil was just right!

GAETA OLIVE SALAD

Insalata Gaeta

It is amazing how one little olive can take you back to another time and place.

INGREDIENTS – SERVES 4

250g Romaine or cos lettuce leaves, washed, dried and chopped
100g radicchio leaves, washed, dried and chopped
1 red onion, finely sliced
100g Gaeta black olives
150g fresh goat's cheese, crumbled
150g cooked cannellini beans *(see recipe on page 209)*, or canned beans (canned beans should be rinsed in a colander and drained well)

INGREDIENTS FOR THE DRESSING

6 tablespoons of extra virgin olive oil
2 tablespoons of white wine vinegar
Salt and pepper

METHOD

- *For the dressing:* Mix together the oil and vinegar, and add salt and pepper to taste.
- Toss the salad leaves, red onion and olives in a bowl with the dressing. Place the beans on top and crumble over the goat's cheese. Serve with warm focaccia bread.

Suggestion: Always dress the salad only a couple of minutes before serving, otherwise the leaves will wilt.

WARM CHICKEN SALAD WITH PANCETTA AND PEPPERS

Insalate di pollo con pancetta e peperoni

Warm salads are enticing in a cold climate.

INGREDIENTS – SERVES 4

250g Romaine or cos lettuce leaves, washed, dried and roughly chopped
100g radicchio leaves, washed, dried and roughly chopped
100g pancetta, thinly sliced
4 radishes, thinly sliced
2 organic or free-range chicken breasts
2 tablespoons of extra virgin olive oil
2 grilled peppers, sliced into strips *(see recipe on page 27)*
Mustard and balsamic dressing *(see recipe on page 82)*

METHOD

- With a sharp knife cut the chicken breast into strips and sauté in the oil, making sure the chicken does not brown.

- Meanwhile grill the pancetta slices on both sides until crisp and set aside on some kitchen paper to absorb the fat.

- Toss the salad leaves, radishes and peppers in a bowl with the dressing.

- Place the chicken and pancetta on top before serving with some warm bread.

WARM GOAT'S CHEESE SALAD WITH WILLIAM PEAR AND WALNUTS

Insalata del Pastore

Reminiscent of the goat herder meandering with his herd while munching on some nuts, pears and fresh cheese.

INGREDIENTS – SERVES 4

250g Romaine or cos lettuce leaves, washed, dried and roughly chopped
50g rocket
4 x 50g slices or wheels of fresh goat's cheese
50g walnuts, crushed
2 mature William pears, peeled and cut into 6 pieces each

INGREDIENTS FOR THE DRESSING

6 tablespoons of extra virgin olive oil
2 tablespoons of balsamic vinegar
1 tablespoon of honey
Salt to taste

METHOD

- *For the dressing:* Mix together the oil, vinegar, honey and salt to taste.
- Pan toast the walnuts briefly on a very hot skillet and set aside.
- Place the goat's cheese on a hot non-stick pan for about 4 minutes until it just starts to melt but still remains intact.
- Meanwhile toss the salad leaves and rocket in a bowl with the dressing. Sprinkle with the walnuts and place the pear on top.
- With a spatula lift the warm goat's cheese, place over the salad and serve immediately with breadsticks.

ORANGE AND FENNEL SALAD

Insalata di arancio con finocchio e olive

Anche l'occhio vuole la sua parte (literally translated – also the eye wants its part) – the aesthetics of a dish play a key role in the culinary arts. This is a wonderful balmy summer's evening salad to serve with fish; it requires an excellent olive oil.

INGREDIENTS – SERVES 4

4 large ready-to-eat oranges, peeled of skin and white pulp and thinly sliced
1 medium fennel, thinly sliced
2 grated carrots
50g taggiasche olives

INGREDIENTS FOR THE DRESSING

4 tablespoons of extra virgin olive oil
Juice of half an orange
Juice of half a lemon
Salt to taste

METHOD

- *For the dressing:* Mix together the oil, orange and lemon juice and salt to taste.
- To prepare the fennel, cut away the fern and stalks (the fern can be used to decorate the salad while the stalks can be used for soups). Cut across the base and remove the outer layer of tough leaves. Slice the rest of the fennel thinly.
- Arrange the slices of orange on a large serving plate and place the fennel slices on top, sprinkle with grated carrot, dot with olives and drizzle with dressing.

PUNTARELLE WITH ANCHOVY SAUCE

Puntarelle con salsa di acciughe

Romans dearly love puntarelle, a variety of Catalonian chicory. During the puntarelle season, lasting from Christmas to Easter, the crispy pale green stalks soaked in anchovy sauce are devoured daily, until finally the stalks turn an unpleasant pale beige and disappear until the following season. It is virtually impossible to find puntarelle outside of Rome. This dish is my daughter Federica's favourite and when we were living in Rome last year I ordered puntarelle daily from a tiny greengrocer on the Viale Aventino where the owner's very old mother spends the entire day preparing vegetables for her son's customers. The vegetables, whether they be puntarelle, artichokes or vegetables for minestrone, were cut and cleaned with an artisan's precision, immersed in large buckets of ice-cold water and subsequently packed into small transparent plastic bags and knotted. We have spent endless hours experimenting with other vegetables to find a suitable accompaniment to the anchovy sauce, and probably broccoli cooked *al dente* is the next best thing.

INGREDIENTS – SERVES 4

600g fresh prepared and washed puntarelle
Anchovy sauce *(see recipe on page 82)*
4 tablespoons of extra virgin olive oil

METHOD

- Make the anchovy sauce.
- *To prepare the puntarelle*: Use only the inner leaves/stalks of the chicory. Cut away the stalk at the base. Cut each tender stalk into thin strips and place in a bowl of iced water. Leave in the cold water for half an hour and they will curl.
- Mix the sauce through the puntarelle along with the oil and serve with fresh crusty bread.

MARCHE BOMBA SALAD

Insalata bomba

This is a substantial salad loved by teenagers. Keep a couple of jars or tins of quality tuna in olive oil in the cupboard. They can make it for themselves or a group of friends.

INGREDIENTS – SERVES 4

  250g mixed salad leaves
  100g radicchio leaves, washed, dried and roughly chopped
  30g rucola/rocket
  320g tuna preserved in olive oil
  200g fresh mozzarella, diced
  12 cherry tomatoes, halved
  12 black olives
  8 tablespoons of extra virgin olive oil
  2 tablespoons of lemon juice or balsamic vinegar

METHOD

- Toss the salad leaves, rocket and tomatoes together in a large bowl and dress with the oil and lemon juice or balsamic vinegar.
- Add the tuna, olives and mozzarella, mix well and serve with toasted ciabatta bread.

DRESSINGS

Condimenti

ANCHOVY SAUCE

Salsa con le acciughe

INGREDIENTS

2 cloves of garlic, peeled

6 salted anchovies

1 teaspoon of white wine vinegar

6 tablespoons of extra virgin olive oil

METHOD

*   With a pestle and mortar pound the anchovies and garlic along with the vinegar and 2 tablespoons of the oil to form a paste. Dilute with the rest of the oil and leave to rest.

Suggestion: Use to dress puntarelle or crunchy broccoli and drizzle on crostini. Anchovy sauce also goes well with mozzarella. Be careful about adding extra salt as anchovies tend to be quite salty.

SALAD DRESSING

Condimento per l'insalata

INGREDIENTS

250ml extra virgin olive oil

80ml balsamic vinegar or white wine vinegar

Pinch of salt

METHOD

*   Shake the ingredients together in a closed jar and use to dress salads.

LEMON DRESSING

Condimento al limone

INGREDIENTS

250ml extra virgin olive oil

Juice of 1 lemon

Pinch of salt

METHOD

*   Shake the ingredients together in a closed jar and use to dress salads and fish.

CITRUS DRESSING

Condimento con gli agrumi

INGREDIENTS

250ml extra virgin olive oil

Juice of half a lemon or lime

Juice of half an orange

½ teaspoon of orange or lemon zest

Pinch of salt

METHOD

*   Shake the ingredients together in a closed jar and use to dress fish.

MUSTARD AND BALSAMIC DRESSING

Condimento con senape

INGREDIENTS

250ml extra virgin olive oil

80ml balsamic vinegar

1 clove of garlic, peeled

1 tablespoon of coarse mustard

1 teaspoon of lemon juice

Pinch of salt

METHOD

- With a mortar and pestle, pound the mustard, garlic, salt and lemon juice along with a little of the oil. Dilute with the rest of the oil and the vinegar and leave to rest.

Suggestions: Serve with warm chicken salad.

BALSAMIC REDUCTION
Riduzione di balsamico

Balsamico tradizionale di Modena is as precious as gold and just a level teaspoon is sufficient to dress a good helping of fresh strawberries. Widely used instead is balsamic vinegar. Source a quality vinegar from Modena without artificial colouring and sweeteners.

INGREDIENTS

250ml balsamic vinegar
2 tablespoons of honey

METHOD

- Simmer the vinegar and honey gently over a low heat in a small heavy-based saucepan for 20 minutes. Leave to rest for a couple of hours before using. You can also add lemon or orange zest, juniper berries or fresh herbs.

Suggestions: Serve with roast meats or drizzle sparingly over pasta dishes with a cream base.

BARBERA WINE REDUCTION
Riduzione di Barbera

INGREDIENTS

300ml Barbera red wine
100ml vegetable broth *(see recipe on page 133)*
1 shallot, finely sliced
2 tablespoons of honey
2 tablespoons of extra virgin olive oil

METHOD

- Gently sauté the shallot in the oil, add the broth, wine and honey, and simmer for 15 minutes until it reduces to a third.

Suggestion: Serve with roast and pan-fried meats.

CREAM OF PARMIGIANO
Fonduta di parmigiano

INGREDIENTS – SERVES 4–6

150ml fresh cream
150ml fresh milk
100g freshly grated parmigiano
Pinch of salt and pepper

METHOD

- In a heavy-based saucepan heat the milk and cream and bring to simmering point. Fold in the parmigiano, salt and pepper to taste and leave to rest for 5 minutes before using.

Suggestion: Use as a dressing for filled pasta such as ravioli with spinach and ricotta, and dot with balsamic reduction.

Pasta & Risotto

I primi piatti

Pasta and risotto are known as *primi piatti* (first plates). Pasta or risotto is served after the antipasto and before the main course. It is common in Italy that if the antipasto is fish, then the pasta or risotto and main course will also be based on fish.

Pasta

Fresh pasta is made daily at our Bar Italia restaurant using 00 flour, which is a very finely ground flour suitable for making pasta. We make tonnarelli, orecchiette, tagliatelle and filled pasta, which is then delivered to our other restaurants. We also use dried pasta from Gragnano (just outside of Naples), considered the home of dried pasta, and dried egg pasta from Campofilone in the Marche. It is very important to use good-quality dried pasta that does not easily overcook and delivers a good bite.

FRESH PASTA
Pasta fresca

INGREDIENTS – SERVES 4–6

400g flour (00 or all-purpose flour)
4 organic or free-range eggs, beaten
Pinch of salt

METHOD

- Dust a large work surface with some extra flour. Pour the 00 or all-purpose flour onto the work surface with a pinch of salt and form a mound.

- Make a well in the middle and pour in the beaten eggs.

- Start to knead the dough by mixing with your fingers and incorporating all of the flour until you form a smooth pliable dough. Mould into a ball, dust with flour and place in a covered bowl in the fridge for 30 minutes or so.

- If you have a pasta machine then pass the dough through at least 5 or 6 times before cutting the required shape. If not, simply roll it out several times for about 5 to 10 minutes, to about ½cm thick, and with a sharp knife cut into tagliatelle-like strips of 2cm wide or pappardelle of 4cm wide.

- Leftover bits or *maltagliate* (badly cut) can be used to add to soups.

RAVIOLI WITH RICOTTA AND SPINACH

Ravioli con ricotta e spinaci

INGREDIENTS – SERVES 4–6

Batch of fresh pasta *(see recipe on page 87)*

For the filling
400g fresh ricotta
400g fresh spinach

100g freshly grated Parmigiano Reggiano
1 egg yolk, beaten
½ teaspoon of lemon zest
Pinch of nutmeg
Salt and pepper to taste

METHOD

- *For the pasta:* Prepare the fresh pasta to the point of forming the dough. Cut the dough into two pieces, mould into two balls and place in a covered bowl in the fridge for an hour or so. Pass each portion of dough through a pasta machine 5 or 6 times, or roll them out into large pasta sheets – it can take 5 to 10 minutes of rolling.

- *For the filling:* Steam the spinach for a couple of minutes until it withers and chop finely, eliminating any liquid in the process. Mix the fresh ricotta with the beaten egg yolk, add the lemon zest, pinch of nutmeg, salt and pepper to taste, then leave to rest for 5 minutes. Fold the spinach and Parmigiano Reggiano into the ricotta mixture.

- Spread one pasta sheet onto a well-floured board. Drop dollops of the filling onto the pastry in a straight line at 6cm intervals (the first dollop should start at 3.5cm from the edge).

- Continue on to rows 2 and 3 and so on with 6cm spacing between the rows. Cover with the second sheet of pastry and press down gently around each dollop to remove the air.

- Cut out neat ravioli squares of 6cm x 6cm, spread them out on a large board and leave to rest for an hour before cooking.

- Cook in plenty of boiling salted water and serve simply with butter and sage, Dunne & Crescenzi tomato and basil sauce *(see recipe on page 93)* or cream of parmigiano *(see recipe on page 83)*.

RAVIOLI WITH SMOKED IRISH SALMON AND ORANGE ZEST

Ravioli con salmone irlandese affumicato con arancio

A fusion of traditional spinach and ricotta ravioli with smoked Irish salmon and Sicilian dressing.

INGREDIENTS – SERVES 4

500g spinach and ricotta ravioli *(see recipe on page 89)*
250g smoked or fresh Irish salmon, shredded
1 shallot, very finely sliced
½ glass of dry white wine
4 tablespoons of extra virgin olive oil
Knob of butter (optional)
Zest of 2 oranges
Juice of half an orange

METHOD

- Sauté the shallot in the oil over a low heat until it becomes translucent, add the salmon and stir.

- Add the wine and cook off the alcohol, then return to a low heat and pour in the orange juice. Simmer for a couple of minutes.

- Meanwhile cook the ravioli in a large saucepan of boiling salted water for 1 minute less than the recommended cooking time and drain.

- Add the ravioli and the orange zest to the warm pan along with the salmon and warm through with a knob of butter if desired. Serve immediately.

Suggestion: Spinach and ricotta ravioli can be sourced from well-stocked supermarkets and delis should you not have time to make them.

SPINACH AND RICOTTA TORTELLI WITH PARMIGIANO CREAM AND BALSAMIC REDUCTION

Tortelli di ricotta e spinaci con fonduta di parmigiano e riduzione di balsamico

Stefano Baglioni from Tuscany and visiting chef at Dunne & Crescenzi uses cream of parmigiano and balsamic reduction extravagantly in pasta dishes. When this one first appeared on the board some customers ordered two plates. My nephews, living in Italy, affectionately call tortelli *dischi volanti* – flying saucers.

INGREDIENTS – SERVES 4

500g fresh spinach and ricotta tortelli
150ml cream of parmigiano *(see recipe on page 83)*
50ml balsamic reduction *(see recipe on page 83)*
50g freshly grated parmigiano
Knob of butter

METHOD

- *For the tortelli:* Prepare the pasta as for ravioli with spinach and ricotta *(see recipe on page 89)* but cut out circles 6cm in diameter instead of squares.

- Gently heat the cream of parmigiano in a wide, heavy-based saucepan.

- Cook the fresh tortelli in plenty of boiling salted water for 2 or 3 minutes, drain and toss in the parmigiano cream with a knob of butter.

- Drizzle with balsamic reduction and sprinkle generously with grated parmigiano. Serve immediately.

DUNNE & CRESCENZI PASTA WITH TOMATO AND BASIL SAUCE

Spaghetti al pomodoro e basilico

People write to us from all over the world, having eaten in the restaurant, to request the recipe for *Pasta al pomodoro*. The response is usually the same – no garlic? no oregano? Italian cooking excels in its simplicity by using a couple of quality ingredients – dried pasta from Gragnano, ripe plum tomatoes from Campania, fresh basil and extra virgin olive oil. We get great satisfaction from seeing children enjoy our food in the restaurant. One of our young customers, Desmond McCarthy, first arrived in the restaurant with his parents as a newborn baby. *Pasta al pomodoro* became his favourite as soon as he could eat. He now enjoys practically everything on the menu and recently we served him his first cappuccino. Very soon Desmond will be asking for ravioli with truffle sauce. (Desmond is already a foodie: he updates me regularly on the quality of his pasta – 'just right', 'not enough sauce'). It is good for children to share adult food and feel part of the whole dining experience.

INGREDIENTS – SERVES 4

400g dried spaghetti from Gragnano
100g freshly grated parmigiano
2 tins of Mediterranean plum
  tomatoes
2 fresh, ripe plum tomatoes, chopped

2 shallots, finely sliced
4 tablespoons of extra virgin olive oil
4 basil leaves
Salt to taste

METHOD

- Sweat the shallots in the oil for about 5 minutes in a large wide pan over a low heat until they become translucent.

- Add the tinned and fresh tomatoes, salt and basil, cover and cook for 15 minutes on a medium heat. Blitz with a hand blender and leave to rest. Meanwhile cook the spaghetti *al dente* in a saucepan of boiling salted water according to the instructions on the packet.

- Drain the pasta in a colander and add to the pan, stir, fold in the freshly grated parmigiano and serve immediately.

SQUID INK PASTA WITH FRUITS OF THE SEA

Linguine al nero di seppia ai frutti di mare

Squid ink is amalgamated into the dough during the pasta-making process, giving it a distinctive fish taste, which is magnified by the fresh seafood sauce. Although we change the menu regularly, we have customers who request this specifically and so the chef always has the ingredients close by.

INGREDIENTS SERVES 4–6

400g dried squid ink pasta
400g mussels, cleaned and cooked *(see recipe on page 41)*
400g clams, cleaned and cooked *(see recipe on page 124)*
200g fresh shelled prawns
2 cloves of garlic, peeled
½ glass of white wine
½ teaspoon of dried chilli flakes
4 tablespoons of extra virgin olive oil
12 cherry tomatoes, halved
Bunch of flat-leaf parsley, chopped

METHOD

- Cook the pasta *al dente* according to the instructions on the packet. While the pasta is cooking, warm the garlic and chilli in the oil over a low heat. Stir in the prawns and tomatoes, add the wine and increase the heat momentarily to cook off the alcohol, then return to a low heat.

- Cover and cook for 2 minutes, add the clams and mussels, along with their strained cooking juices, and continue to cook for an additional 2 minutes. Drain the pasta and add to the seafood saucepan, stir and sprinkle with parsley, and serve immediately.

    Suggestion: It is imperative to have a reliable fishmonger who can supply you with fresh fish and who will clean and cut the fish as you require.

STROZZAPRETI WITH AUBERGINES, PINE NUTS, SPECK AND CHERRY TOMATOES

Strozzapreti con melanzane, pinoli, speck e pomodorini

Strozzapreti means choke the priest – not for some vindictive reason but rather that the pasta is so good your guest will wolf it down and run the risk of choking!

INGREDIENTS – SERVES 4–6

400g dried spaghetti from Gragnano
200g speck (a smoked variant of prosciutto), thinly sliced
100g freshly grated parmigiano
25g Mediterranean pine nuts
½ glass of white wine

2 aubergines
16 cherry tomatoes, halved
8 tablespoons of extra virgin olive oil
2 cloves of garlic, peeled
Salt

METHOD

* Peel and slice the aubergines thickly and place on a tray. Sprinkle with salt and leave for 30 minutes, then rinse off the salt, pat dry and dice.

* Pan toast the pine nuts on a hot skillet for one minute and set aside.

* Sauté the garlic, aubergines and speck in the oil for 2 minutes, add the tomatoes and cook for another 2 minutes.

* Pour in the wine and increase the heat momentarily to cook off the alcohol, then return to a low heat, add a quarter cup of boiling water, cover and cook slowly for 15 minutes.

* Meanwhile cook the pasta *al dente* in plenty of salted water. Drain the pasta and add to the pan and stir. Sprinkle with the pine nuts and plenty of parmigiano and serve.

Suggestions: This is also good with a dollop of fresh ricotta. Omit the speck for vegetarian guests.

FETTUCCINE WITH SALMON AND COURGETTE

Fettuccine con salmone e zucchine

Pasta with cream and smoked salmon was very much in vogue during the boom years of the 1960s and popular with the Dolce Vita set who thronged the bars and restaurants of Via Veneto in Rome.

INGREDIENTS – SERVES 4–6

400g fresh fettuccine or dried pasta from Gragnano
250g fresh salmon fillet, cut into chunks, or smoked Irish salmon, sliced
125ml fresh cream
100ml milk
2 shallots, finely sliced
1 courgette, diced
4 tablespoons of extra virgin olive oil
½ glass of dry white wine
¼ teaspoon of lemon zest
Knob of butter (optional)

METHOD

- Cook the fettuccine or Gragnano pasta *al dente* according to the instructions on the packet and drain. Meanwhile sauté one shallot in a little of the oil and add the courgette, stir and add a couple of tablespoons of boiling water (from the pot where the pasta is cooking), cover and cook for 5 minutes.

- In another wide saucepan, sauté the other shallot slowly in the rest of the oil over a low heat. Add the salmon and stir, add the wine and increase the heat momentarily to cook off the alcohol, then return to a low heat.

- Add the cream and milk and simmer for 5 minutes. Stir in the shallot and courgette mixture, the lemon zest and the butter if required. Add the pasta to the pan, mix lightly and serve immediately.

Suggestions: A drop of brandy can be used instead of wine, and penne are also good with this sauce.

BUCATINI PASTA WITH GUANCIALE AND TOMATO

Bucatini all'amatriciana

Bucatini all'amatriciana is another dish the Romans have laid claim to. Originally from the town Amatrici in northern Lazio, it consisted of guanciale and Pecorino and no tomato. A true Roman *bucatini all'amatriciana* will be deprived of onion, chilli, wine and garlic, but consist of flavoursome guanciale (cured pork cheek) and freshly grated Roman Pecorino cheese. This is Stefano's family recipe and it's how we prepare it in the restaurant.

INGREDIENTS – SERVES 4–6

400g bucatini pasta

100g guanciale (or pancetta), diced

100g freshly grated Pecorino Romano cheese

500ml tomato passata or 2 tins of plum tomatoes (mash the plum tomatoes with a fork before using)

4 tablespoons of red wine vinegar

8 tablespoons of extra virgin olive oil

Salt to taste

METHOD

- Cook the bucatini in plenty of salted boiling water for 1 minute less than the recommended cooking time.

- Meanwhile take a wide saucepan and sauté the guanciale in the oil over a low heat, allowing the guanciale to release its juices into the oil but avoid crisping it.

- Add the vinegar and increase the heat for a couple of seconds, then add the tomato and salt and cook for 15 minutes, stirring occasionally.

- Drain the pasta and transfer to the saucepan with the sauce, mix and fold in the Pecorino Romano cheese and serve immediately.

Suggestion: Bucatini are thick spaghetti-like tubes and the sauce tends to go everywhere. You might want to warn your guests! Once the pasta has been eaten the remaining sauce can be soaked up with chunks of bread known as scarpetta – little shoe; this is perfectly acceptable when dining.

PACCHERI PASTA FROM GRAGNANO WITH DUBLIN BAY PRAWNS AND TOMATO

Paccheri di Gragnano con gamberi e pomodoro

Paccheri are our favourite shape of pasta for fish. The square tubes are perfect hosts for prawns and tomato.

INGREDIENTS – SERVES 4–6

400g dried paccheri pasta from
    Gragnano
400g shelled Dublin Bay prawns
250ml tomato passata
2 cloves of garlic, peeled
½ teaspoon of dried chilli flakes
½ glass of dry white wine

8 tablespoons of extra virgin olive oil
1 carrot
1 onion
1 celery stick
Bunch of flat-leaf parsley, finely
    chopped
Salt

METHOD

- Prepare a light fish stock by simmering the heads and shells removed from the prawns, along with the carrot, onion and stick of celery in a saucepan of salted water for 10 minutes.

- Strain the liquid from the fish broth and discard the rest.

- Sauté the garlic and chilli on a gentle heat in the oil.

- Add the prawns and pour in the wine. Increase the heat momentarily to cook off the alcohol, then return to a low heat and add the tomato and 150ml of the fish stock. Cover and simmer for 5 minutes.

- Meanwhile cook the paccheri pasta *al dente*, according to the instructions on the packet. Drain and add to the sauce.

- Toss and serve immediately with the chopped parsley sprinkled over it.

Suggestion: Crushed pistachios can be added to this dish to give it an interesting texture.

PAPPARDELLE WITH DUCK AND VINSANTO

Pappardelle con anatra profumate al vinsanto

Tuscany is the home of pappardelle (a wide fettuccine type of pasta). This is usually served with a *selvaggina* game sauce. The name pappardelle comes from the word *pappare*, to eat, and in fact *pappa* is an endearing term for food as in *La pappa dei bambini*, meaning baby food.

INGREDIENTS – SERVES 4–6

400g pappardelle pasta
2 skinless duck breasts, diced
2 shallots, finely sliced
4 tablespoons of extra virgin olive oil
100ml vinsanto dessert wine
150ml fresh cream
100ml milk
A sprig of thyme
Pinch of nutmeg

METHOD

- Sweat the shallots and thyme in the oil over a low heat. Remove the thyme with a slotted spoon.
- Add the duck breast, stir to absorb the pan juices and pour in the vinsanto. Increase the heat momentarily to cook off the alcohol, then return to a lower heat.
- Add the nutmeg, cream and milk, and simmer for 10 minutes.
- Meanwhile cook the pasta *al dente* according to the instructions on the packet, drain and add to the saucepan, stir and serve immediately.

Suggestion: While duck lends itself to white sauces, it's not so good with tomato.

PENNE WITH TOMATO, GARLIC AND CHILLI

Penne all'arrabbiata

Arrabbiata, meaning angry or fired up, is assigned to this simple Roman pasta dish because it is fired up with hot chilli flakes. As young students we used to make this at midnight and discuss politics until dawn.

INGREDIENTS – SERVES 4–6

400g dried penne pasta from Gragnano
500ml tomato passata or 2 tins of plum tomatoes (mash the tinned tomatoes with a fork before using)
4 cloves of garlic, peeled
12 tablespoons of extra virgin olive oil
1 tablespoon of flat-leaf parsley, finely chopped
1 level teaspoon of chilli flakes

METHOD

- In a wide saucepan gently sauté the garlic and chilli in the oil – avoid browning the garlic.
- Add the tomato, cover and cook for 10 minutes over a medium heat, stirring occasionally. If you are using tinned tomatoes, blend them into the sauce with a wooden spoon. Should the sauce become dry add a couple of tablespoons of boiling water from the pasta pot.
- Meanwhile, cook the penne pasta in a large saucepan of boiling salted water, according to the instructions on the packet, but drain the pasta in a colander 1 minute before the recommended cooking time.
- Add the pasta to the pan, stir, sprinkle with the parsley and serve immediately.

Suggestion: Quick and easy to make, this dish hits the spot when you are ravenously hungry.

LA CARBONARA

RIGATONI ALLA CARBONARA
Rigatoni alla carbonara

Rigatoni alla carbonara is so simple, yet takes a lot of practice to master, hence many restaurants resort to adding cream. The skill is in managing the eggs – not too runny and not scrambled; it's about timing and rhythm and using organic eggs and guanciale (cured pork cheek). Guanciale perfumes the oil it's cooked in with wonderful peppery herbs, and the taste of this permeates through the eggs.

INGREDIENTS – SERVES 4–6

400g dried rigatoni pasta from Gragnano
200g guanciale, thinly sliced
100g freshly grated Parmigiano Reggiano
100g freshly grated Pecorino Romano
5–7 organic eggs yolks, beaten (or one egg per person plus one extra)
10 tablespoons of extra virgin olive oil
Freshly ground black pepper

METHOD

- Fold half of the Pecorino Romano and half of the Parmigiano Reggiano into the eggs, along with a dash of black pepper.

- In a wide, heavy-based saucepan gently heat the guanciale in the oil – be careful not to crisp the guanciale, it must release its flavours into the oil.

- Meanwhile cook the rigatoni *al dente*, according to the instructions on the packet, and drain.

- Add the pasta to the pan (the heat should be off) and stir and coat the pasta with the guanciale oil, then pour over the eggs while stirring gently to create a cream. Serve immediately with the rest of the Pecorino and Parmigiano.

Suggestion: Packaged pancetta does not give the same results as artisanal guanciole. You can, however, marinate the pancetta for an hour in a little olive oil along with plenty of freshly ground black pepper and a sprig of rosemary and then use.

SCHIAFFONI WITH ASPARAGUS, MONKFISH AND THYME

Schiaffoni con asparagi, coda di rospo e timo

The silky smooth surface of schiaffoni invites the sauce to wrap around the pasta rather than be absorbed.

INGREDIENTS – SERVES 4–6

400g schiaffoni or dried paccheri pasta from Gragnano
400g monkfish fillets, cut into chunks
250g fresh asparagus tips
1 sprig of fresh thyme
1 clove of garlic, peeled
½ teaspoon of dried chilli flakes
½ glass of dry white wine
6 tablespoons of extra virgin olive oil
100ml vegetable broth *(see recipe on page 133)*
Salt

METHOD

- Cook the asparagus in a saucepan of simmering salted water for a couple of minutes, then drain and dice.

- Sauté the garlic, thyme and chilli in the oil, stir in the monkfish, add the wine and increase the heat momentarily to cook off the alcohol, then return to a low heat. Pour in the vegetable broth, cover and cook for 5 minutes.

- Gently fold in the asparagus and cook for 2 minutes.

- Meanwhile cook the pasta in a large saucepan of boiling salted water, according to the instructions on the packet, but for 1 minute less than the recommended cooking time.

- Drain the pasta and add to the sauce. Serve immediately.

PENNE WITH PECORINO CHEESE AND BLACK PEPPER

Penne cacio e pepe

This dish, although simple, needs practice to get it just right; the art is in forming the cream. Two simple ingredients, Pecorino Romano cheese and pepper, when worked well, can give spectacular results. Restaurants, regardless of poor atmosphere or terrible service, feature in prominent food guides to Italy based on the quality of their *cacio e pepe*. Romans will travel vast distances to eat the best *cacio e pepe*.

INGREDIENTS – SERVES 4–6

400g dried penne pasta from Gragnano
200g grated Pecorino Romano cheese
1 tablespoon of freshly ground black pepper
Salt

METHOD

- Cook the penne in plenty of boiling salted water for 1 minute less than the recommended cooking time.
- Drain, but retain a cup of the cooking water, and transfer the pasta to a large warm serving bowl along with 2 tablespoons of the cooking water.
- Fold in the Pecorino cheese and black pepper while stirring gently; the cheese and liquid should form a nice cream.
- If it is too moist add more Pecorino Romano or if too dry add another spoonful of water. Serve immediately.

Suggestion: Tonnarelli is my preferred pasta for cacio e pepe *but chefs insist on using penne.*

TONNARELLI WITH GENOVESE PESTO, POTATO AND STRING BEANS

Tonnarelli al pesto Genovese con patate e fagiolini

When we opened our first deli in Sutton an elderly neighbour came to buy pesto every other day. After a couple of months, I politely commented on how much she must love pasta with pesto. 'Oh no,' she replied, 'I cream it through my mashed potatoes.' My neighbour used the pesto to enhance her mashed potatoes. In this dish the Genovese, on the other hand, use potatoes to enhance pasta with pesto.

INGREDIENTS – SERVES 4–6

400g tonnarelli pasta
200g freshly grated Tuscan Pecorino
200g string beans
1 medium potato, peeled
4 heaped tablespoons of fresh Genovese pesto *(see recipe on page 55)*
Salt

METHOD

- Dice the potato quite small and cook in boiling water, drain and set aside.
- Cook the string beans *al dente* in boiling water, drain and set aside.
- Put the pesto in a small bowl and place it over a pot of simmering water to heat.
- Cook the tonnarelli pasta in plenty of salted boiling water for 1 minute less than the recommended cooking time and drain.
- Transfer the pasta to a large warm serving bowl, stir in the potato, string beans, warm pesto and plenty of freshly grated Tuscan Pecorino cheese and serve.

Suggestion: Genovese pesto is a speciality from Liguria. Should you decide to buy commercial pesto, dilute with a tablespoon of water from the pasta pot.

ORECCHIETTE
Basic recipe for Orecchiette

Orecchiette (meaning little ears, but don't let that put you off!) is typical of Puglia, and customers love orecchiette served with broccoli or broccoli and *salsiccia* (sausage) *(see recipe on page 119).*

INGREDIENTS

200g 00 flour
100g semolina durum wheat
Tepid water
Salt

METHOD

- Mix the semolina, flour and a little salt together in a bowl and turn out onto a floured board.
- Make a well in the middle and add enough tepid water to form a dough, knead and roll into a long snake of 2.5cm thick.
- Forming the orecchiette takes practice. Slice the roll (1cm) and at the same time pull the slice towards you with a knife, sort of rolling it towards you.
- Place each slice on your thumb like a little hat to form the orecchiette. Spread the batch on a board and sprinkle with semolina, cover with a clean dry cloth and leave in a cool place.

ORECCHIETTE WITH BROCCOLI AND SALSICCIA

Orecchiette con broccoli e salsiccia

INGREDIENTS – SERVES 4–6

400g dried or fresh orecchiette pasta *(see recipe on page 117)*
600g broccoli, washed
250g fresh salsiccia sausage
8 cherry tomatoes, halved
2 cloves of garlic, peeled
4 tablespoons of extra virgin olive oil
½ level teaspoon of chilli flakes
½ glass of dry white wine
Salt

METHOD

- Cook the broccoli in just enough salted water to cover it until soft. Remove the broccoli with a slotted spoon, place in a bowl and mash with a fork, retaining the cooking water.

- Bring the broccoli water back to boiling point, add the orecchiette and cook for about 8 minutes for dried or 3 minutes for fresh.

- Meanwhile scrape the sausage meat from the skin and sauté along with the tomatoes, garlic and chilli flakes in the oil.

- Add the wine and increase the heat momentarily to cook off the alcohol, then return to a low heat. Continue to cook over a low heat for 5 minutes.

- Now add the cooked broccoli along with a couple of tablespoons of broccoli water and cook for a further 5 minutes.

- Drain the orecchiette, add to the pan, stir and serve.

Suggestion: To cater for vegetarian guests simply eliminate the sausage and sprinkle with freshly grated Pecorino cheese or mature ricotta and black pepper before serving.

ORECCHIETTE WITH ARTICHOKES

Orecchiette con carciofi

Every town and village throughout Italy hosts a food and wine festivity known as a *sagra* almost weekly. A new crop of seasonal vegetables is typically celebrated with a *sagra*. For example the *sagra* of the artichoke consists of stalls being set up all around the town with people cooking and selling everything that can be made from artichokes – pasta dishes, preserves, pesto, artichokes fried, braised and roasted. Orecchiette are the perfect shape to host flavoursome chunks of artichoke.

INGREDIENTS – SERVES 4–6

400g dried or fresh orecchiette pasta *(see recipe on page 117)*
150ml vegetable broth *(see recipe on page 133)*
100g grated Pecorino cheese
2 braised artichokes, cooked *(see recipe on page 201)*
1 tablespoon of flat-leaf parsley, finely chopped
Salt

METHOD

- Chop the cooked artichokes roughly and place in a saucepan along with the vegetable broth. Cover and simmer for five minutes.

- Cook the orecchiette *al dente* in plenty of boiling salted water.

- Drain the orecchiette and add to the pan, stir and serve with the parsley and grated Pecorino.

Suggestion: Alternatively for a creamy sauce you can blitz the sauce with a hand blender and add a couple of tablespoons of cream.

GNOCCHI

Basic recipe for gnocchi

Gnocchi are a kind of potato dumpling dressed with a variety of sauces, just like pasta. They are found in different shapes and forms throughout Italy and you can be sure to find gnocchi on the menu of most small traditional trattorie or family-owned restaurants.

INGREDIENTS – SERVES 8–10

1kg floury potatoes
300g plain flour
1 organic or free-range egg yolk
1 tablespoon of white wine or prosecco

METHOD

- Boil the potatoes in their jackets. Once cooked remove the fluffy potatoes from their skins, mash and mix with the flour.

- Place the mixture on a floured wooden board and make a well in the middle.

- Add the egg yolk and wine and mix lightly with your fingers to form a soft dough.

- Now for the fun part: make long snakes with the dough (just like when you were a kid at school) 1½cm thick.

- Cut into small 3cm logs. Rub each gnocco along the back of a fork to give it a nice linear pattern.

Suggestion: Children love making gnocchi and they can have fun adding some herbs, cooked spinach or a little beetroot to create different colours.

GNOCCHI WITH HAZELNUT SAUCE

Gnocchi con crema di nocciole

Hazelnuts are widely used in Italian cooking, from desserts such as nutella (created by Ferrero in response to American peanut butter) to savoury pasta and risotto dishes. Hazelnut sauce adds a touch of sophistication to the gnocchi.

INGREDIENTS – SERVES 8–10

400g gnocchi *(see recipe on page 122)*
250g peeled hazelnuts
150ml fresh cream
100ml fresh milk
100g freshly grated parmigiano
2 tablespoons of extra virgin olive oil
Salt and ground black pepper

METHOD

- Blitz the nuts and oil in a food mixer.
- Warm the cream and milk in a saucepan and stir in the blended nuts along with some parmigiano and salt to taste.
- Meanwhile cook the gnocchi in a large saucepan of boiling salted water, and when they rise to the surface drain in a colander.
- Place on a warm serving dish, cover with the sauce and serve immediately with freshly ground black pepper.

Suggestion: You can also use walnuts instead of hazelnuts.

GNOCCHI WITH PORCINI MUSHROOMS AND CLAMS

Gnocchi mare e monti

The Marche area of Italy, where we have a home and spend some time, has one of the most interesting and diverse culinary palettes of Italy. The area is separated from Umbria and Tuscany by the Apennine mountain range and continues across the gentle Sibelline hills down to the Adriatic sea. Food from the Marche tends to offer up an eclectic mix of seafood (*mare*) and forest or hillside foods (*monti*).

INGREDIENTS – SERVES 4–6

400g gnocchi *(see recipe on page 122)*
100g dried porcini mushrooms
250g fresh clams
½ cup of vegetable stock *(see recipe on page 133)*
½ cup of dry white wine

2 cloves of garlic, peeled
Bunch of flat-leaf parsley, finely chopped
½ teaspoon of chilli flakes
4 tablespoons of extra virgin olive oil
Salt and freshly ground pepper

METHOD

- Soak the porcini mushrooms in a mug of tepid water with a drop of milk, and leave for at least an hour.

- Steep the clams in a basin of cold water and change the water several times over. If any are open tap them on the side of a plate and they should close – if not, discard.

- Sauté 1 clove of garlic and the chilli in half of the oil, add the clams and the wine, increase the heat momentarily to cook off the alcohol, then return to a low heat, cover and cook for a couple of minutes until all of the clams have opened.

- Meanwhile drain the porcini from the liquid and shred. Sauté the other clove of garlic in the rest of the oil in a saucepan and add the porcini and vegetable stock, then cook for a couple of minutes.

- Meanwhile cook the gnocchi in a large saucepan of boiling salted water until they rise to the surface, and drain. Add the gnocchi to the mushroom saucepan along with the clams and juice, mix and serve immediately with parsley, salt and freshly ground pepper to taste.

Suggestion: You can use mussels instead of clams.

GNOCCHI WITH FOUR CHEESE SAUCE
Gnocchi ai quattro formaggi

The diner should be able to distinguish the four cheeses of a good *quattro formaggi*.

INGREDIENTS – SERVES 4

400g gnocchi *(see recipe on page 122)*
100g Gorgonzola cheese, crumbled
80g Fontina cheese
80g Talleggio cheese, cut into cubes
80g grated parmigiano
200ml milk
50ml fresh cream
Salt and freshly ground pepper

METHOD

- Soak the Fontina cheese in the milk for 2 hours.

- Then in a heavy-based saucepan warm the milk with the Fontina, add the fresh cream, fold in the rest of the cheese and stir continuously until the cheese has melted and blended into a creamy consistency.

- Cook the gnocchi in plenty of boiling salted water and once they rise to the surface, drain and place in a large serving dish and cover with the creamy cheese sauce.

- Add freshly ground pepper and salt to taste. Serve immediately.

Suggestion: This sauce is stunning with freshly grated truffle if you can get your hands on some, but a couple of drops of truffle oil stirred into the sauce is nice too.

GNOCCHI WITH KERRY LAMB RAGÙ

Gnocchi al ragù di agnello

To our good fortune about a year ago we were contacted by Michael Gottstein on behalf of the Ring of Kerry lamb group and he wanted to know if we would take their lamb for the restaurant. The Ring of Kerry lambs are mostly grass fed, are free to roam around the local hills, are ethically treated and there is traceability from farm to fork. We have never looked back.

INGREDIENTS – SERVES 4–6

400g gnocchi *(see recipe on page 122)*
400g minced lean lamb
100g freshly grated parmigiano
500ml tomato passata or 2 cans of
    plum tomatoes
Soffritto of 1 diced carrot, stick of
    celery and shallot

2 ripe beef tomatoes, chopped
1 glass of red wine
1 small sprig of rosemary
4 bay leaves
4 tablespoons of extra virgin olive oil
Salt and freshly ground black pepper

METHOD

- Sauté the soffritto on a low heat in the oil, add the meat and stir until it becomes deep pink (but avoid browning). Add the wine and increase the heat momentarily to cook off the alcohol, then return to a low heat.

- Add the tomatoes, rosemary, bay leaves, salt and pepper. Cover and cook for 2 hours. Stir occasionally and add a little boiling water should the sauce start to dry up.

- Cook the gnocchi in a large saucepan of salted boiling water, until they rise to the surface.

- Drain and place in a wide serving dish, pour over the ragù with plenty of freshly grated parmigiano and serve.

Suggestion: This ragù is also good with short tube-shaped pasta.

TRADITIONAL LASAGNA
Lasagna tradizionale

We call this traditional lasagna because each region of Italy boasts its own lasagna based on local ingredients, from the famous *lasagna Bolognese* with the classical Bolognese sauce to the Vincisgrassi of the Marche with chicken giblets. In Naples lasagna tends to incorporate whatever lies in the fridge, from boiled eggs to ends of salami. Over the last ten years we have introduced forty different types of lasagna to the restaurant and *lasagna tradizionale* remains one of our best-sellers. Last year I was speaking to a group of young students in Rome and asked what their favourite Sunday lunch consisted of. I was surprised at the response – *lasagna della nonna naturalmente*, followed by roast veal and potatoes. A good lasagna is light enough to permit the eating of two portions!

INGREDIENTS – SERVES 6–8

400g dried lasagna
200g grated parmigiano
200g quality minced beef
200g quality minced pork
200g mozzarella, diced
50g pancetta, diced
500ml tomato passata or 2 tins of
plum tomatoes

2 ripe beef tomatoes, chopped
Soffritto of 1 diced carrot, stick of
celery and 2 shallots
1 glass of red wine
6 tablespoons of extra virgin olive oil
2 bay leaves
Salt and pepper to taste

INGREDIENTS FOR WHITE SAUCE (BÉCHAMEL)

50g butter
50g plain flour

500ml milk

METHOD

- *For the ragù:* Sauté the soffritto in the oil on a low heat and add the pancetta, cook for a couple of minutes and add the minced meats. Stir until the meat takes on a rich pink colour but avoid browning. Add the wine and increase the heat momentarily to cook off the alcohol, then add the tomatoes, bay leaves, salt and pepper to taste, and cook on a low heat for about 2 hours, stirring occasionally. Add some warm water if it becomes dry.

- *For the béchamel sauce:* Melt the butter, and stirring continuously fold in the flour little by little until it is absorbed. Gradually pour in the milk, little by little, stirring continuously until all of the milk is absorbed and the sauce coats the back of a spoon.

- *To assemble:* Preheat the oven to 200 degrees. Put a little oil in the bottom of a rectangular oven dish and line with lasagna sheets.

- Cover with a thin layer of ragù, drizzle béchamel sparingly over the ragù, sprinkle with the parmigiano and dot with the mozzarella.

- Repeat this process for about three or four layers, finishing with a layer of béchamel, parmigiano and mozzarella. Place in the oven for around 40 minutes.

- Leave to rest for a couple of minutes before cutting.

Suggestion: Make double the quantity of ragù and use as a sauce for rigatone or gnocchi.

LASAGNA WITH SMOKED IRISH SALMON AND SPINACH
Lasagna con salmone irlandese affumicato e spinaci

My Aunt Jean and my Uncle Mario, a *simpatico* Roman, have spent the best part of the last forty years sourcing ingredients throughout Italy and cooking for family and friends. They are probably the first foodies I knew. Jean introduced this lasagna, based on smoked Irish salmon, to the Irish community living in Rome and we brought it home through the restaurant.

INGREDIENTS – SERVES 6–8

400g dried lasagna
200g grated parmigiano
500g fresh spinach, washed and
    ready to use
250g smoked Irish salmon
2 tablespoons of extra virgin olive oil
Knob of butter

1 bay leaf
250ml fresh cream
250ml fresh milk
2 shallots, diced
½ glass of white wine
Béchamel sauce *(see recipe on page 129)*
Salt

METHOD

- Preheat the oven to 200 degrees.

- Blanch the spinach in boiling salted water for a minute and drain very well. Soak the bay leaf in the milk.

- Sweat the shallots in the oil and butter over a gentle heat and stir in the smoked salmon.

- Add the wine and increase the heat momentarily to cook off the alcohol, then return to a low heat. Pour in the cream and milk, bring to simmering point and leave to rest. Remove the bay leaf with a slotted spoon.

- Place a little oil in the bottom of a rectangular oven dish. Line the bottom with lasagna sheets and cover with a thin layer of the salmon cream, drizzle sparingly with some béchamel, dot with spinach and sprinkle with parmigiano.

- Repeat this process for about three layers, finishing with a layer of béchamel and parmigiano. Place in the oven for around 40 minutes.

Suggestion: Leave to rest for five minutes before cutting.

LASAGNA WITH PORCINI MUSHROOMS

Lasagna con funghi porcini

In Italy saints' name days are celebrated just like a birthday and if you are fortunate enough to have a saint's name you get to celebrate twice every year. In our family we celebrate Santo Stefano, St Stephen's Day, with *lasagna con funghi porcini*.

INGREDIENTS – SERVES 6–8

400g dried lasagna sheets or 600g
    fresh lasagna sheets
200g grated parmigiano
200g dried porcini mushrooms
1 glass of white wine
2 tablespoons of extra virgin olive oil

2 shallots, diced
250ml fresh cream
250ml fresh milk
Knob of butter
Béchamel sauce *(see recipe on page 129)*

METHOD

- Preheat the oven to 200 degrees.

- Soak the porcini mushrooms in the milk for around 2 hours. Remove and shred the mushrooms and strain the milk.

- Sweat the shallots in the oil and butter and stir in the mushrooms.

- Pour in the wine and increase the heat momentarily to cook off the alcohol, then return to a low heat. Pour in the milk and cream, bring to simmering point and leave to rest.

- Line the bottom of an oiled rectangular oven dish with lasagna sheets and cover with a layer of mushroom cream, drizzle sparingly with some béchamel and sprinkle with parmigiano.

- Repeat this process for about three layers, finishing with a layer of mushroom cream. Place in the oven for around 40 minutes. Leave to rest for a couple of minutes before cutting.

Suggestion: We do another version with saffron. Dissolve a sachet of saffron in a little warm milk and add to the béchamel sauce.

Risotto

While rice is a popular grain enjoyed by most populations in a multitude of dishes, risotto is indigenous to Italy. Northern Italy is dotted with rice paddies stretching from Piedmont to Lombardy to Veneto.

The most common grains of rice suitable for risotto would be vialone nano, carnaroli or arborio, and these provide the best risotto results. At Dunne & Crescenzi we use either carnaroli or vialone nano depending on the dish – carnaroli for creamy risotto and vialone nano for moist risotto such as our risotto with quail or risotto with butternut squash. These types of rice absorb the broth without easily overcooking and at the same time release starch, which in turn creates a nice creamy risotto with a bite to it. Arborio is the more commonly known rice variety for risotto and is widely available, but some supermarkets are increasingly stocking carnaroli and vialone nano.

Cooking risotto is a labour of love; it requires patience and attention, consisting of adding broth to the rice, ladle by ladle, allowing each ladle of broth to be absorbed before adding the next and so on, and stirring gently for about 20 minutes.

Butter, contrary to general belief, is widely used in northern Italy. Adding unsalted butter to a risotto to enhance the creamy consistency is called *mantecare*. But if you prefer to avoid butter just eliminate it from the recipe; the risotto will still be very good but not as creamy.

A good risotto is dependent on the quality of the broth, and at the restaurant we make three types of broth daily – fish broth, vegetable broth and meat broth. We have chosen not to use chicken broth as we feel that chicken broth tends to overpower the main protagonists in the risotto.

In the recipes I advise 1½ litres of broth but you will not necessarily use all of it. Each recipe is different depending on the ingredients – just keep adding the broth until the rice is cooked *al dente*. On the other hand should you finish the broth, top up with boiling water. Remember that the broth is already salty, so always taste your risotto before adding more salt!

Finally, risotto must be served immediately otherwise it will continue to absorb the juices and very quickly become stodgy.

THE BROTH

Il Brodo

VEGETABLE BROTH

INGREDIENTS
1½ litres of cold salted water
2 whole onions, peeled
2 whole carrots, washed
2 celery sticks, washed
Freshly ground pepper
Parsley
Salt

METHOD
- Immerse all of the ingredients in a pot of cold water, cover and simmer for 30 minutes. Strain the broth into another pot ready for use.

MEAT BROTH

INGREDIENTS
1½ litres of cold salted water
2 whole onions, peeled
2 whole carrots, washed
2 celery sticks, washed
4 whole ripe beef tomatoes
250g stewing beef, trimmed of fat
4 bay leaves
Bunch of parsley

Freshly ground pepper
Salt

METHOD
- Immerse all of the ingredients in a pot of cold water, cover and simmer for 90 minutes. Strain the broth into another pot ready for use.

FISH BROTH

INGREDIENTS
1½ litres of cold salted water
2 whole onions, peeled
2 whole carrots, washed
2 celery sticks, washed
Head and bones of one large white fish such as seabream, monkfish or turbot, along with 1 kg of the shells and heads of prawns
Bunch of parsley
Freshly ground pepper

METHOD
- Immerse all of the ingredients in a pot of cold water, cover and simmer for 30 minutes. Strain the broth into another pot ready for use.

RISOTTO WITH PRAWNS AND COURGETTES

Risotto con gamberi e zucchine

Risotto con gamberi e zucchine features on the restaurant board to celebrate St Patrick's Day because of the green, white and orange colours it combines.

INGREDIENTS – SERVES 4–6

320g carnaroli rice
16 king prawns or Dublin Bay prawns, cleaned and shelled
2 courgettes, diced
2 shallots, finely sliced
8 tablespoons of extra virgin olive oil
60g butter for creaming
Knob of butter
1 glass of dry white wine
1½ litres of fish broth *(see recipe on page 133)*
1 handful of flat-leaf parsley, finely chopped
Salt and pepper to taste

METHOD

- Sauté the shallots in 4 tablespoons of oil and a knob of butter slowly over a low heat until they soften and become translucent, add the courgettes and stir. Add the rice and allow it to absorb the flavours in the pot for about 2 minutes (in Italy this is called toasting).

- Now add the wine and increase the heat momentarily to cook off the alcohol, then return to a low heat. Add the fish broth ladle by ladle, waiting for each ladle to be absorbed – it takes around 20 minutes until the rice is cooked.

- Meanwhile in the rest of the oil sear the prawns, a minute on each side, and add to the risotto just before it's ready.

- *Mantecare* or cream the risotto by folding in the butter, salt and pepper as desired and sprinkle with the parsley. Serve immediately.

Suggestion: Local Dublin Bay prawns play a key role in this risotto.

TUSCAN SAUSAGE AND CABBAGE RISOTTO

Risotto con salsicce e cavoli

Tuscan black cabbage is wonderful but, since it is hard to come by, Savoy cabbage is used in the restaurant.

INGREDIENTS – SERVES 4–6

320g carnaroli rice
4 salsicce (Tuscan sausages)
2 shallots, finely sliced
½ head of Savoy cabbage, washed
    and cut into ribbons
60g butter for creaming
6 tablespoons of extra virgin olive oil

1 glass of white wine
1½ litres of vegetable broth *(see
    recipe on page 133)*
1 sprig of fresh rosemary
100g freshly grated parmigiano or
    Tuscan Pecorino

METHOD

- Blanch the cabbage for a couple of minutes in boiling water, drain and discard the water.

- Scrape the sausage meat from the skin and crumble into a saucepan along with 2 tablespoons of the oil, the rosemary and the cabbage.

- Stir and cook over a low heat for 3 to 4 minutes until the cabbage wilts, but do not allow the sausage to brown. Remove the rosemary and discard.

- Sauté the shallots in the rest of the oil in another heavy-based saucepan. Add the rice and leave to absorb the flavours of the saucepan for about 2 minutes, then add the cooked sausage, cabbage and juices.

- Pour in the wine and increase the heat momentarily to cook off the alcohol, return to a low heat and begin adding the vegetable broth ladle by ladle, stirring continuously for about 20 minutes or until the rice is cooked *al dente*.

- Cream the risotto with the butter and fold in plenty of parmigiano or Tuscan Pecorino.

- Serve immediately.

Suggestion: You can make a similar risotto with radicchio from Treviso (salsicce con radicchio Trevisano) instead of cabbage; you don't need to blanch the radicchio and should keep some aside for decoration.

MUSHROOM RISOTTO WITH PARMIGIANO PETALS

Risotto ai funghi con petali di parmigiano

Fresh porcini mushrooms are a delicacy in Italy and widely consumed, particularly in the autumn months. Best sliced thick and grilled, porcini are loved for their distinctive nutty flavour, meaty texture and irresistible smell. They can, however, be difficult to source in Ireland, but quality dried porcini mushrooms can give good results.

INGREDIENTS – SERVES 4–6

320g carnaroli rice
150g champignon mushrooms
100g dried porcini mushrooms
100g grated parmigiano
100g parmigiano shavings
60g butter for creaming

4 tablespoons of extra virgin olive oil
1½ litres of vegetable broth (*see recipe on page 133)*
2 shallots, finely sliced
1 glass of dry white wine
2 tablespoons of milk

METHOD

- Place the porcini mushrooms in a bowl and cover with tepid water and 2 tablespoons of milk and leave aside for about an hour.

- Remove the mushrooms from the liquid with a slotted spoon, then strain the liquid and set aside for use in the risotto.

- Slice the champignon mushrooms thinly and shred the porcini.

- Sauté the shallots in the oil slowly over a low heat until they become translucent.

- Add the porcini and champignon mushrooms followed by the rice and stir.

- Pour in the wine, increase the heat momentarily to cook off the alcohol, then return to a low heat.

- Add the porcini juice and start adding the vegetable broth ladle by ladle for about 20 minutes until the rice is cooked.

- Fold in the grated parmigiano and butter.

- Sprinkle with the parmigiano shavings and serve immediately.

RISOTTO WITH RED CABBAGE AND ROBIOLA CHEESE
Risotto al cavolo rosso e robiola

Soft and creamy robiola cheese mellows the red cabbage.

INGREDIENTS – SERVES 4–6

320g carnaroli or vialone nano rice
400g red cabbage washed and chopped small
100g parmigiano cheese
100g fresh robiola cheese
60g butter for creaming
1 litre of vegetable broth *(see recipe on page 133)*
Knob of butter
4 shallots, finely sliced
2 glasses of full-bodied red wine (preferably Barbera d'Asti)
4 tablespoons of extra virgin olive oil
Salt and pepper

METHOD

- Sauté the shallots in the oil and a knob of butter over a low heat until they soften, add the red cabbage and leave to cook slowly until it wilts.

- Add the rice and allow it to absorb the juices in the saucepan, add the wine and increase the heat momentarily to cook off the alcohol, then return to a low heat.

- Add the vegetable broth, ladle by ladle, for about 20 minutes, stirring continuously until the rice is cooked.

- Cream with the butter and parmigiano and gently fold in the robiola, lots of freshly ground pepper, and salt to taste.

- Serve immediately.

Suggestion: You can use fresh ricotta instead of robiola.

RISOTTO WITH GRAPPA, QUAIL, SAFFRON AND RADICCHIO

Risotto alla grappa con petti di quaglia, zafferano e radicchio

For thirty years Stefano's family spent three months of every summer in the Val di Non, Trentino. They rented the same house year after year as is common in Italy. Nonna Valentina was very fond of enriching her sauces with the local grappa, a liquor distilled from the stalks and seeds of grapes. Saffron generally features a lot on our menu – it adds an exotic taste to food and a wonderful burst of colour.

INGREDIENTS – SERVES 4–6

320g vialone nano rice
100g radicchio leaves, shredded
8 quails (ask the butcher to skin them and remove the breasts)
2 shallots, finely sliced
½ glass of grappa
1½ litres of vegetable broth *(see recipe on page 133)*

50g freshly grated Grana Trentino cheese
60g butter for creaming
6 tablespoons of extra virgin olive oil
1 sachet of saffron
Sprig of thyme
Salt and pepper to taste

METHOD

- Pound the quail breasts, cut into thin strips and set aside for the risotto. You can add the rest of the quail to the vegetable broth and simmer for 20 minutes.

- Sauté the shallots in the oil until they become translucent, add the quail breasts and thyme, stir, pour in the grappa and increase the heat momentarily to cook off the alcohol, then return to a low heat.

- Cover and cook for a couple of minutes, then remove the thyme with a slotted spoon. Add the rice and stir. Then begin to add the broth, ladle by ladle, stirring continuously for 15 minutes.

- Dissolve the saffron in a ladle of the broth and stir into the risotto along with the radicchio and cook for a further 5 minutes or until the rice is cooked. At this point fold in the Grana and butter, salt and pepper to taste and serve.

Suggestion: Try exchanging the quail for hare or rabbit, which is very good indeed.

RISOTTO WITH CREAM OF SCAMPI

Risotto alla crema di scampi

Risotto alla crema di scampi is a best-seller in the restaurant and a family favourite.

INGREDIENTS – SERVES 4–6

320g carnaroli rice

1½ litres of fish broth *(see recipe on page 133)*

600g Dublin Bay prawns, cleaned and shelled

60g butter for creaming

Knob of butter

800g fresh cream

2 shallots, finely sliced

150ml tomato passata

6 tablespoons of extra virgin olive oil

1 glass of brandy

1 clove of garlic

Bunch of flat-leaf parsley

Salt and pepper

METHOD

- Warm the garlic in 2 tablespoons of the oil, then remove with a slotted spoon.

- Add the prawns to the oil, pour in the brandy and increase the heat to cook off the alcohol, then return to a low heat (put aside 4–6 prawns, depending on servings, for decoration), add the tomato, salt and a hint of pepper and cook over a low heat for 5 minutes.

- Place the prawns and juices in a blender along with the cream and give it a quick blitz.

- Meanwhile sauté the shallots in the rest of the oil and a knob of butter, add the rice and leave to absorb the juices in the saucepan, then start to add the fish broth, ladle by ladle, stirring continuously for about 15 minutes until almost cooked.

- Fold in the prawn cream and a ladle of broth, and cook for another 5 minutes, then cream with the butter and decorate with the parsley and a whole prawn per serving.

RISOTTO WITH FRUITS OF THE SEA

Risotto ai frutti di mare

Risotto ai frutti di mare is usually translated as seafood risotto but I particularly love the Italian idea of seafood being fruits from the sea and decided to call it that.

INGREDIENTS – SERVES 4–6

320g carnaroli rice
500g fresh clams
250g cuttlefish, roughly chopped
250g fresh mussels, scrubbed and
   de-bearded
500g fresh prawns, shelled
12 tablespoons of extra virgin olive
   oil
8 cherry tomatoes, cut in half

4 cloves of garlic, peeled
Bunch of flat-leaf parsley, roughly
   chopped
1 teaspoon of chilli flakes
½ teaspoon of lemon zest (optional)
1½ litres of fish broth *(see recipe on
   page 133)*
1½ glasses of dry white wine

METHOD

- Discard any broken or open clams and place the rest in a large basin of cold water (I like to add a little salt to the water), leave for a couple of hours and over that time rinse the clams three or four times by changing the water.

- In a separate basin treat the mussels in the same way.

- In a wide, heavy-based saucepan sauté a clove of garlic and ½ teaspoon of chilli flakes in 4 tablespoons of the oil. Drain the water from the clams and add them to the pan.

- Pour in ½ glass of wine, increase the heat momentarily to cook off the alcohol, then return to a low heat, cover and shake the pan a couple of times. After 4 minutes remove the cover from the pan and start to discard any clams that have not opened. Remove from the heat, strain the juice and conserve for the risotto.

- In another saucepan repeat the same operation with the mussels. Remove from the heat, strain the juice and conserve for the risotto.

- In a third heavy-based saucepan sauté the cuttlefish, 2 cloves of garlic, cherry tomatoes and lemon zest in the remaining oil. Add ½ glass of wine and increase the heat momentarily to cook off the alcohol, then return to a low heat.

- Add the juice from the mussels and clams and leave to simmer for 5 minutes. Now add the rice and leave to absorb the flavours from the saucepan.

- Begin to add the fish broth, ladle by ladle, stirring continuously for 20 minutes until the rice is almost cooked. In a skillet sear the prawns on both sides in a little extra oil and add to the risotto along with the clams and mussels.

- Sprinkle with the parsley and serve immediately.

Suggestion: In Italy this risotto is served with a side plate to discard the shells. You might prefer to remove the fish from the shells before adding to the risotto.

RISOTTO WITH SCALLOPS AND FENNEL
Risotto con scaglie di capesante e finocchio

The delicious and powerful anise flavour of the fennel sweetens when cooked and merges nicely with the scallops.

INGREDIENTS – SERVES 4–6

320g vialone nano or carnaroli rice
(I prefer vialone for this one)
8 scallops
2 cloves of garlic, peeled
2 shallots, finely sliced

6 tablespoons of extra virgin olive oil
½ fennel bulb, sliced wafer-thin
1 glass of dry white wine
1½ litres of fish broth *(see recipe on page 133)*

METHOD

- Gently fry the garlic in 2 tablespoons of the oil, add the scallops and seal on both sides, then cook for a further 2 minutes and remove from the oil.

- Leave to cool, then slice the scallops thinly with a sharp knife.

- Sauté the shallots in the rest of the oil slowly over a low heat until they become translucent, stir in the fennel and add the rice, followed by the wine, and increase the heat momentarily to cook off the alcohol, then return to a low heat.

- Add the fish broth, ladle by ladle, for about 20 minutes, stirring continuously.

- Fold in the scallops and serve.

RISOTTO WITH RADICCHIO, GORGONZOLA AND WALNUTS

Risotto radicchio, Gorgonzola e noci

Radicchio Trevigiano from Treviso is an elongated radicchio and milder in flavour than the round one. It melts into the risotto like a pink cream but you can use either variety for this recipe.

INGREDIENTS – SERVES 4–6

320g carnaroli or vialone nano rice
80g Gorgonzola cheese, crumbled
50g crushed walnuts
60g butter for creaming
100g freshly grated parmigiano
1½ litres of vegetable broth *(see recipe on page 133)*

1 medium head of red radicchio, washed and cut into ribbons
2 shallots, finely sliced
1 glass of dry white wine
4 tablespoons of extra virgin olive oil
Knob of butter
Salt and pepper

METHOD

- Toast the crushed walnuts briefly on a very hot skillet and set aside.
- Sauté the shallots over a low heat in the oil and a knob of butter until they soften, add half of the radicchio and leave to cook for a good 5 minutes until it wilts, add the rice and allow to absorb the juices of the saucepan.
- Add the wine and increase the heat momentarily to cook off the alcohol, then return to a low heat. Now add the vegetable broth, ladle by ladle, for about 20 minutes, stirring gently until the rice is cooked *al dente*.
- Add the walnuts and the rest of the radicchio and cook for another couple of minutes. Fold in the crumbled Gorgonzola with the butter for creaming and parmigiano.
- Add salt and pepper as desired.
- Serve immediately.

Suggestion: You can use hazelnuts, pine nuts or pistachio nuts instead of walnuts.

RISOTTO WITH BUTTERNUT SQUASH, SPECK AND GRANA TRENTINO

Risotto con zucca, speck e Grana Trentino

The use of butternut squash in pastas and risottos has seen a revival of late. Formerly associated with the *cucina povera* or peasant cuisine it is now widely appreciated and associated with fine dining.

INGREDIENTS – SERVES 4

320g vialone nano rice
250g speck, thinly sliced
800g butternut squash
60g butter for creaming
100g freshly grated Grana Trentino cheese
1 glass of dry white wine

1½ litres of vegetable broth *(see recipe on page 133)*
2 shallots, finely sliced
6 tablespoons of extra virgin olive oil
Knob of butter
Salt and pepper to taste

METHOD

- Cut the butternut squash lengthways, discard the seeds and place on a roasting tin, drizzle with 2 tablespoons of the oil and place in a hot oven for 15 minutes, then remove from the oven and mash the pulp with a fork.

- Take a heavy-based saucepan and sauté the shallots in the rest of the oil and a knob of butter slowly over a low heat until the shallots become translucent.

- Now add the speck and coat in the oil but do not allow to brown, follow with the glass of wine and increase the heat momentarily to cook off the alcohol.

- Return to a low heat. Add the rice and coat in the juices.

- Stir in the butternut squash and start to add the vegetable broth slowly ladle by ladle, stirring continuously for about 20 minutes or until the rice is cooked *al dente*.

- Add an extra ladle of broth at this point as this risotto should be nice and moist.

- Cream with the butter and Grana Trentino cheese, and add salt and pepper to taste.

- Serve immediately.

RISOTTO WITH BAROLO

Risotto al Barolo

An indulgent and luxurious risotto.

INGREDIENTS – SERVES 4–6

320g vialone nano rice
200g crumbled Castelmagno or Gorgonzola cheese
50g freshly grated parmigiano
4 tablespoons of extra virgin olive oil
1 litre of meat or vegetable broth *(see recipe on page 133)*
½ litre of Barolo wine
4 shallots, finely sliced
Salt and pepper to taste

METHOD

- Sauté the shallots in the oil over a low heat until translucent, add the rice and stir to absorb the flavours of the saucepan.
- Add the Barolo little by little until it becomes absorbed, continue the same process with the broth adding ladle by ladle, stirring continuously for about 20 minutes.
- Add salt and pepper to taste.
- Fold in the cheese and serve immediately.

Suggestion: You can use any good full-bodied red wine but avoid oaky or young red wines.

RISOTTO WITH CREAM OF ASPARAGUS AND PECORINO

Risotto con crema di asparagi e Pecorino

At the restaurant, this risotto usually announces the arrival of spring. Use a mild Pecorino – the Roman variety is too salty for a risotto.

INGREDIENTS – SERVES 4–6

320g vialone nano or carnaroli rice
400g fresh asparagus tips
60g butter for creaming
150g Pecorino sheep's cheese – 100g grated and 50g shaved
150ml fresh single cream

3 shallots, finely sliced
1 glass of dry white wine
1½ litres of simmering vegetable broth *(see recipe on page 133)*
4 tablespoons of extra virgin olive oil
Salt and pepper to taste

METHOD

- Sauté 2 shallots on a low heat in 2 tablespoons of the oil until they become translucent.

- Add the rice and leave it to absorb the flavours of the saucepan. Add the wine and increase the heat for half a minute to cook off the alcohol, then return to a low heat.

- Continue cooking over a low heat, adding the hot broth, ladle by ladle, stirring gently for about 20 minutes.

- Meanwhile in another saucepan sweat 1 shallot in the rest of the oil over a low heat and add the fresh asparagus along with a couple of spoons of vegetable broth, cover and cook for 3 minutes.

- Put aside a couple of asparagus tips for decoration and place the rest along with the pan juices in a blender with the fresh cream and blitz quickly.

- Fold the asparagus cream into the risotto when it is *al dente* and cook for another couple of minutes. Cream by folding in the butter and grated Pecorino cheese.

- Add salt and pepper as desired, decorate with Pecorino flakes and asparagus, and serve immediately.

Suggestion: Add a bunch of asparagus stalks to the broth to enhance the flavour.

Main Courses

I Secondi Piatti

Main courses of meat and fish are called *secondi piatti* (second plates) and they are served after the *primi piatti*. Side orders of vegetables called *contorni* are generally served on separate plates so that the flavours don't become tainted by the ingredients of the main course. Remember when you are ordering food in a restaurant in Italy that you must select the main course and the side order; it doesn't automatically accompany the mains.

PAN-FRIED HAKE WITH CHERRY TOMATOES

Nasello in padella sul letto di pomodorini

Fish in Italy is usually cooked in all its glory with the head intact. The fish is gutted and stuffed with some parsley, garlic and lemon, and oven baked, then dressed with local olive oil and freshly squeezed lemon juice. Here we have a preference for fish ready to eat and nicely presented.

INGREDIENTS – SERVES 4–6

4 x 200g fresh hake fillets
½ glass of dry white wine
4 tablespoons of extra virgin olive oil
¼ teaspoon of lemon zest
1 sprig of fresh thyme

1 clove of garlic, peeled
4 small bunches of cherry tomatoes
   on the vine
Salt and pepper to taste

METHOD

- Gently heat the garlic and thyme in the oil in a wide, non-stick, heavy-based saucepan and then remove with a slotted spoon. Stir in the lemon zest and place the fillets skin down on the pan.

- Pour in the wine and increase the heat momentarily to cook off the alcohol, then return to a low heat. Cover and continue to cook for 3 to 4 minutes, then add salt and pepper to taste.

- Meanwhile take each bunch of cherry tomatoes and score the tops close to the vine.

- Blanch each bunch in boiling water for a couple of minutes and drain. Remove the skin of each tomato but keep the bunch intact on the vine.

- Place a fillet of fish on the vines and drizzle with good extra virgin olive oil.

- Serve with chickpeas or chickpea cream *(see recipe on page 209)*.

Suggestion: Preparing the tomatoes is time-consuming, so you can simply slice 16 cherry tomatoes in half and add to the oil along with the lemon zest. Heat for one minute before adding the fish fillets.

CALAMARI FILLED WITH RICOTTA AND PISTACHIO NUTS FROM BRONTE

Calamari ripieni di ricotta e pistacchi di Bronte

Sicilian Bronte pistachio nuts add an interesting texture to the creamy ricotta-filled calamari which we enjoyed in Salina, one of the Aeolian Islands off the coast of Sicily.

INGREDIENTS – SERVES 4–6

8 fresh calamari cleaned (ask your fishmonger to do this for you)

250g fresh ricotta cheese

100g crushed Bronte pistachio nuts

2 tablespoons of finely chopped marjoram

1 egg yolk

1 clove of garlic, peeled

1 teaspoon of lemon zest

½ glass of dry white wine

6 tablespoons of extra virgin olive oil

8 cherry tomatoes, halved

Salt and pepper to taste

METHOD

- For the filling, mix together the ricotta, pistachios, egg yolk, marjoram, lemon zest, and salt and pepper to taste.

- Remove the head and tentacles from the calamari (you can use these for fish broth).

- Place some filling inside each of the calamari and close the ends with toothpicks.

- Take a wide, heavy-based saucepan and sauté the garlic in the oil, add the tomatoes and cook for a couple of minutes, then add the calamari and seal on both sides. Pour in the wine, cover and cook over a low heat for 15 minutes.

- Serve warm or at room temperature.

Suggestion: Cooking calamari is all about timing: it has to be just right, too little or too much and your calamari will be like rubber. It's those couple of precious in-between minutes that will determine the dish, and this comes with experience. If a calamari is really fresh 10–15 minutes should be correct. Test and if it's tough then just add some warm water and continue cooking for another 5 minutes.

SICILIAN COUSCOUS

Cuscusu Siciliano

Sicilians have made this North African dish their own, based on local seafood, Bronte pistachio nuts and salted anchovies.

INGREDIENTS – SERVES 4–6

240g ready-to-use quality couscous

1 litre of fish broth *(see recipe on page 133)*

4 salted anchovies

2 whole small fresh fish, like cod or sea bream, cleaned and scaled

500g mussels

25g Bronte pistachio nuts, shelled and crushed

25g Sicilian raisins

½ glass of dry white wine

Soffritto of 1 finely diced shallot, carrot and stick of celery

500ml tomato passata or 2 cans of plum tomatoes

2 cloves of garlic, peeled

Bunch of flat-leaf parsley, finely chopped

Pinch of nutmeg

Pinch of cinnamon

Salt and pepper to taste

METHOD

- Prepare and cook the mussels *(see recipe on page 41)* then remove the mussels from their shells and set aside.

- Over a gentle heat sauté the soffritto along with the garlic, anchovies and parsley.

- Add the whole fish and pour in the wine, increase the heat momentarily to cook off the alcohol, then lower the heat again.

- Add the tomato, a couple of spoons of fish broth, salt, pepper, cinnamon and nutmeg, cover and simmer for 20 minutes. Strain the sauce and remove the fish from the bones. Return the sauce to the heat and add the fish, mussels and raisins.

- Meanwhile prepare the couscous with the rest of the fish broth, according to the instructions on the packet. Pour the prepared couscous onto a large serving dish and cover with the fish sauce.

- Sprinkle with the pistachio nuts.

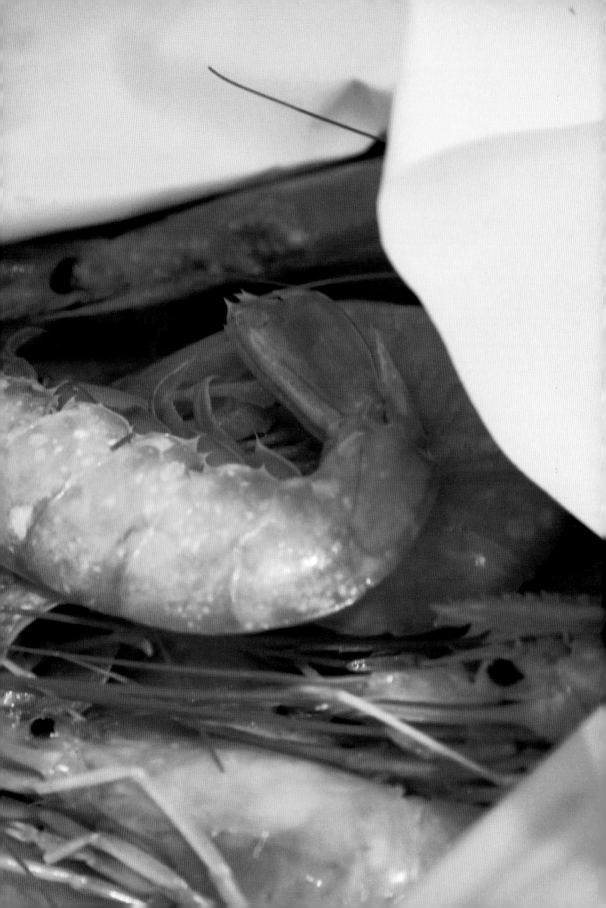

KING PRAWNS WITH CITRUS AND ZIBIBBO SAUCE
Mazzancolle con salsa di agrumi e zibibbo

Zibibbo is a wonderful dessert wine with complex citrus and apricot flavours which enhance the prawns.

INGREDIENTS – SERVES 4

16 shelled king prawns
A little plain flour for coating the prawns
1 clove of garlic, peeled
Zest of 1 lemon
Juice of 1 lemon
4 tablespoons of extra virgin olive oil
1 espresso cup of zibibbo liquor (from Sicily)
Knob of butter (optional)

METHOD

- Lightly coat the prawns in flour.
- Warm the garlic in the oil, then remove with a slotted spoon.
- Seal the prawns on both sides in the oil.
- Add the zibibbo and increase the heat momentarily to cook off the alcohol, then lower the heat and pour over the lemon juice and zest, add the butter and cover for a couple of minutes.
- Serve with spinach with cream of parmigiano *(see recipe on page 202)*.

Suggestion: You can use brandy if you don't have zibibbo.

PARCELS OF IRISH SALMON WITH CITRUS SAUCE

Filetto di salmone irlandese in cartoccio con salsa di agrumi

Citrus sauce lends a Mediterranean exotic touch to our Irish salmon.

INGREDIENTS – SERVES 4

4 fillets of fresh Irish salmon
Zest of 1 orange
Zest of 1 lemon
Juice of ½ orange
Juice of ½ lemon
2 tablespoons of extra virgin olive oil
Knob of butter (optional)

METHOD

- Preheat the oven to 180 degrees.
- Rub a little oil on 4 sheets of greaseproof paper and place a fillet of salmon on the middle of each sheet.
- Mix the lemon and orange zest together with the juices and spoon this dressing onto the fish.
- Dot with a little butter and close the parcels by loosely pleating the top and crimping the edges.
- Bake in the oven for 15 minutes or until the fish is ready.
- Serve the parcels along with string beans with balsamic dressing *(see recipe on page 203)*.

FISH PARCELS WITH CHERRY TOMATOES, CAPERS AND OLIVES

Pesce in cartoccio con pomodorini, capperi e olive

Cooking in parcels ensures that the fish absorbs the intense flavours of the condiment and remains nice and moist. Sea bream, sea bass, cod, haddock, salmon and halibut are all delicious cooked in parcels.

INGREDIENTS – SERVES 4

4 x 200g fresh fish fillets
100g taggiasche olives
1 tablespoon of capers, rinsed and drained
4 tablespoons of extra virgin olive oil
4 tablespoons of white wine
8 cherry tomatoes, halved
4 fresh basil leaves

METHOD

- Preheat the oven to 180 degrees.
- Rub a little extra oil on 4 sheets of greaseproof paper and place a fillet of fish on the middle of each sheet.
- Spoon over each a tablespoon of oil and wine, a couple of cherry tomatoes, a leaf of basil and some capers and olives.
- Seal the parcels by loosely pleating the top and crimping the edges.
- Bake in the oven for 10 minutes or until the fish is ready and serve with courgettes with leeks, raisins and pine nuts *(see recipe on page 204)*.

SEA BASS WITH BLACK OLIVE AND POTATO CRUST

Spigola in crosta di olive nere e patate

Black olive tinges the fish with a burst of flavour while the potato lends substance.

INGREDIENTS – SERVES 4

4 thick fillets of fresh sea bass
4 tablespoons of black olive pesto *(see recipe on page 53)*
2 medium potatoes, peeled
6 tablespoons of extra virgin olive oil
Juice of 2 lemons
Salt to taste

METHOD

- Preheat the oven to 180 degrees.

- Slice the potatoes wafer thin (use a mandolin if you have one) and pat dry.

- Drizzle a baking tin with the oil.

- Spread 2 tablespoons of black olive pesto on each fillet of fish, then layer the potatoes on top.

- Place the fillets in the baking tin and cook for 15 minutes or until the potato is nice and crispy.

- Dress with lemon juice, salt to taste and serve.

Suggestion: Cook turbot this way and try an artichoke pesto instead of olive.

SQUID, PEAS AND POTATO STEW

Calamari con patate e piselli

Un piatto unico, meaning that the fish and vegetables are cooked together to form a substantial one-course meal.

INGREDIENTS – SERVES 4

600g squid, cleaned and cut into strips (ask your fishmonger to do this)
350g frozen or fresh peas
250ml tomato passata
2 medium potatoes, diced
4–5 fresh mint leaves
6 tablespoons of extra virgin olive oil
12 cherry tomatoes, halved
1 glass of dry white wine
2 cloves of garlic, peeled
2 shallots, finely sliced
¼ teaspoon of chilli flakes
100ml simmering water
Salt and pepper to taste

METHOD

- Sweat the shallots gently in the oil until they become translucent.
- Add the garlic, cherry tomatoes and chilli and stir, then add the squid and pour in the wine.
- Increase the heat momentarily to cook off the alcohol, then return to a low heat.
- Pour in the tomato passata and simmering water, add pepper and salt to taste, cover and cook for 15 minutes.
- Now add the potatoes, mint and peas (if using frozen peas boil them for five minutes and drain before adding) and cook for an additional 10 minutes.
- Serve with thick slices of bruschetta drizzled with extra virgin olive oil.

  Suggestion: Serve warm rather than hot, drizzled with extra virgin olive oil from Puglia.

POT-ROASTED RABBIT
Coniglio alla cacciatora

Popularly known as Hunter's Rabbit and so-called because hunters, prone to rising with the dawn, would take along a large dish wrapped in a tea cloth and have it for mid-morning breakfast.

INGREDIENTS – SERVES 4

1 rabbit ready to use and cut into
    8 pieces (ask your butcher to do
    this for you)
2 bay leaves
Sprig of rosemary
8 cherry tomatoes halved
6 tablespoons of extra virgin olive oil

3 cloves of garlic, peeled
¼ teaspoon of chilli flakes
4 anchovies (optional)
8 taggiasche olives
4 tablespoons of balsamic vinegar
500ml simmering salted water

METHOD

- In a wide, heavy-based saucepan heat the garlic, chilli and herbs in the oil.
- Add the anchovies and stir until they dissolve in the oil.
- Add the tomatoes, cover and cook for a couple of minutes.
- Add the rabbit, stir and coat with the pan juices.
- Spoon in the vinegar and increase the heat momentarily.
- Add the olives and pour in the water, cover and cook over a gentle heat for 30 to 40 minutes.
- Serve with refried broccoli *(see recipe on page 207)*.

Suggestion: The juices of this dish are good as a sauce for pappardelle pasta. Simply cook the pappardelle according to the instructions on the packet, drain and place in a warm serving bowl. Pour over some rabbit cacciatore juices along with some good olive oil and sprinkle with freshly grated Pecorino. Stefano likes to prepare his pot roast with half chicken and half rabbit or wild hare.

VEAL LIVER WITH SHALLOTS, VENETIAN STYLE

Fegato alla Veneziana

Diners who generally shun liver can be won over with *Fegato alla Veneziana*.

INGREDIENTS – SERVES 4

4 thin slices of veal liver
A little plain flour for coating the liver
6 tablespoons of extra virgin olive oil
4 shallots, finely sliced
6 tablespoons of balsamic vinegar or red wine vinegar
4 fresh sage leaves, chopped

METHOD

- Lightly flour the liver.
- Gently fry the shallots and sage in the oil until they just start to brown.
- Add the vinegar and momentarily increase the heat.
- Place the liver slices flat on the pan, cover and cook for 2 minutes, turn over and cook for a further 2 to 3 minutes.
- Serve with the juice.

Suggestions: When I cook this at home I add the zest of 2 mandarins, which blends beautifully with balsamic vinegar. Veal liver is excellent with braised artichokes.

SIENESE SAUSAGE AND BEAN CASSEROLE
Salsiccia con fagioli

Fresh meaty sausage, succulent, immersed in red wine and hearty beans reminds me of the Vendemmia, grape-picking season in Tuscany.

INGREDIENTS – SERVES 4–6

500g fresh Sienese (or Tuscan) sausage (without fennel)
250g cooked borlotti beans *(see recipe on page 209)* or 1 x 250g tin of borlotti beans
4 bay leaves
4 ripe beef tomatoes, chopped

1 small sprig of rosemary
1 glass of Sangiovese red wine
6 tablespoons of extra virgin olive oil
Soffritto of 1 finely diced shallot, carrot and stick of celery
Salt and freshly ground pepper to taste

METHOD

- Chop the sausage into 4cm pieces.

- Take a wide, heavy-based saucepan and sauté the soffritto in the oil on a low heat. Add the sausage, stir and pour in the wine.

- Increase the heat momentarily to cook off the alcohol, then return to a low heat and add the tomatoes, rosemary and bay leaves, cover and cook for 30 minutes.

- Now add the beans (if you use tinned beans be sure to rinse and drain before using) and continue to cook over a low heat for a further 10 minutes.

- Add salt and pepper to taste, but be careful as the sausage is salty. Serve with big chunks of toasted farmhouse loaf.

Suggestion: For a leaner casserole prick the sausages and plunge into boiling water for a couple of minutes to remove the fat before chopping.
Lentil and sausage casserole: *This is traditionally eaten at midnight on New Year's Eve, purportedly to ensure an adequate supply of money throughout the following year. Prepare as for Sienese sausage and bean casserole and use lentils instead of borlotti beans. First cook the lentils according to the recipe on page 210, then add in place of the beans.*

TWICE-COOKED POLPETTE
Polpette ripassate in padella

These polpette (or rissoles) are little gems of tender goodness. I have particularly fond memories of making these with Nonna Valentina in Val di Non (Trentino). It was the first time I met her and I felt I had to prove myself as a valid partner for her favourite grandson. Valentina normally spoke with a very special loud voice but during this particular event she lowered her voice to a mere whisper: 'The secret is in the frying, not too hot and not too long.'

INGREDIENTS – SERVES 4

400g finely minced beef, preferably organic
50g freshly grated parmigiano cheese
Yolk of one organic or free-range egg
Drop of grappa (optional)
150ml extra virgin olive oil
1 small shallot, very finely sliced
1 cup of breadcrumbs
1 small sprig of thyme
1 small sprig of rosemary
1 level teaspoon of salt and freshly ground black pepper
A little plain flour for coating

INGREDIENTS FOR THE SAUCE

Soffritto of 1 finely diced shallot, carrot and stick of celery
4 basil leaves
500ml tomato passata or 2 tins of plum tomatoes (mash the tinned tomatoes
    with a fork before using)
4 ripe beef tomatoes, chopped
4 tablespoons of extra virgin olive oil
Salt to taste

METHOD

- Combine the meat, shallot, egg, breadcrumbs, grappa, salt and pepper together in a bowl, and mix until well blended.

- Turn onto a floured board and flatten to about 2cm thick.

- Take a 6cm cutter and proceed to cut out the polpette.

- Coat both sides in flour and then heat the oil with the thyme and rosemary in a pan and seal the polpette on both sides for 2 minutes.

- Remove and place on some kitchen paper to soak off the oil.

- Meanwhile prepare the sauce.

- Sauté the soffritto in the oil in a wide saucepan, add the tomatoes, basil and salt, and cook over a low heat for 5 minutes, stirring occasionally.

- Now take the polpette and carefully drop them into the sauce, cover and cook for 15 minutes, shaking the saucepan from time to time.

- Remove the polpette from the sauce with a slotted spoon and serve as a main course with mushrooms with garlic and parsley *(see recipe on page 204)* or red cabbage *(see recipe on page 206).*

Suggestions: The polpette are served as a main course along with some vegetables or salad. Avoid serving the polpette with pasta, although the sauce can be used to dress pasta – rigatoni are particularly good along with plenty of grated parmigiano. Spaghetti and meatballs is the American version and Italians dislike the negative interpretation of Italian culture and cuisine often associated with this dish.

VEAL STEAKS WITH PROSCIUTTO AND SAGE

Saltimbocca

Saltimbocca or 'jump in the mouth' is so good that everyone will want more. A simple recipe based on the perfect combination of prosciutto, veal and a hint of sage.

INGREDIENTS – SERVES 4

4 x 150g tender veal steaks (pound if necessary)
4 wafer-thin slices of prosciutto
4 fresh sage leaves
10 tablespoons of extra virgin olive oil
Knob of butter
½ glass of dry white wine
Salt and freshly ground black pepper
Plain flour for coating

METHOD

- Place a slice of prosciutto and a sage leaf on each veal steak and secure with a toothpick.
- Lightly coat in a little flour.
- Warm the oil in a wide saucepan and seal the steaks on both sides.
- Add the wine and increase the heat momentarily to cook off the alcohol, lower the heat and add the knob of butter.
- Cook for another 2 minutes on both sides.
- Remove the steaks, place on warm plates and pour over the pan juices. Add salt and pepper to taste, but remember the prosciutto is salty. Serve immediately with rosemary roast potatoes *(see recipe on page 207)*.

Suggestion: For best results the dish must be prepared just before dining and served immediately. The toothpicks can be removed before serving if you wish.

CHICKEN ROULADE WITH MORTADELLA, SPINACH AND PINE NUTS

Involtini di pollo con mortadella, spinaci e pinoli

Mortadella is a typical preserved pork sausage or salumi from Bologna. Flavoured with pepper, herbs, pistachio nuts and spices, it makes an ideal ingredient for savoury roulades and panini. Once heated the fat melts and releases the flavours.

INGREDIENTS – SERVES 4

4 chicken breasts (ask your butcher to butterfly them)
500g fresh spinach
25g Mediterranean pine nuts
4 slices of mortadella (or 2 large slices cut in half)

4 basil leaves
8 cherry tomatoes halved
2 shallots, finely sliced
4 tablespoons of extra virgin olive oil
¼ teaspoon of lemon zest
½ glass of dry white wine

METHOD

- Cover the chicken breasts with greaseproof paper and pound with a meat mallet.
- Blanch the spinach in boiling water for 2 minutes and drain very well.
- Pan toast the pine nuts for a minute on a hot skillet.
- Line the chicken breasts with a slice of mortadella and a thin layer of spinach and dot with pine nuts.
- Roll the chicken and secure with a couple of toothpicks.
- Sweat the shallots over a gentle heat in the oil, add the lemon zest, tomatoes and basil and cook for 5 minutes.
- Seal the chicken roulades all over, then pour in the wine, increase the heat momentarily to cook off the alcohol, cover and cook over a gentle heat for 20 minutes.
- Shake the pot from time to time and sprinkle with some more pine nuts before serving.
- Serve with spinach with cream of parmigiano *(see recipe on page 202)* and rosemary roast potatoes *(see recipe on page 207)*.

CHICKEN WITH YELLOW PEPPERS AND BLACK OLIVES

Pollo con peperoni gialli e olive nere

Mediterranean peppers are shiny and oddly shaped; yellow peppers are streaked with beautiful shades of green, tantalising the shopper and the artist.

INGREDIENTS – SERVES 4–6

1 whole organic or free-range chicken, chopped into 8 pieces (if preferred ask your butcher to remove the skin for you)
8 black taggiasche olives
2 cloves of garlic, peeled
1 sprig of fresh rosemary
4 fresh basil leaves
4 medium yellow bell peppers
12 cherry tomatoes halved
4 tablespoons of extra virgin olive oil
½ glass of dry white wine
250ml simmering water or as required
Salt and freshly ground black pepper

METHOD

- Cut the peppers in half, remove the white pulp, slice into thin strips and braise in a hot pan for about 4 minutes, turning them over now and then.

- Meanwhile in a large, heavy-based saucepan warm the garlic, olives, tomatoes and rosemary in the oil.

- Add the chicken and stir, then add the wine and increase the heat for a moment to cook off the alcohol, then return to a low heat. Fold in the peppers followed by the simmering water, basil, salt and pepper.

- Cover and simmer for 45 minutes, checking regularly, and add more simmering water if it starts to dry.

- Serve the chicken pieces drizzled with peppers and sauce.

Suggestion: This tastes better when it is left to riposare or rest and served warm with a simple bruschetta.

BRAISED LAMB SHANKS WITH BALSAMIC AND RED WINE REDUCTION

Stracotto di agnello al forno con riduzione di vino rosso e balsamico

Stracotto (overcooked) describes a meat that is roasted, stewed (*stufato*) or braised (*brasato*) for several hours in a full-bodied wine and herb sauce until it becomes melt-in-the-mouth tender. In Piedmont *stracotto* is usually accompanied by a good Barbera or Barolo wine.

INGREDIENTS – SERVES 4 ABUNDANTLY

4 lamb shanks, trimmed of fat
½ kilo of cherry tomatoes, halved
2 cloves of garlic, crushed
2 cloves of garlic, peeled
½ bottle of full-bodied red wine like Barbera d'Asti

½ glass of wine for deglazing
4 tablespoons of extra virgin olive oil
150ml balsamic reduction (*see recipe on page 83*)
Generous sprig of rosemary

METHOD

- Preheat the oven to 180 degrees. In a pestle and mortar, pound the crushed garlic, some of the rosemary and a tablespoon of the oil.

- Make some incisions here and there in each lamb shank and stuff with the rosemary and garlic paste.

- Drizzle the rest of the oil into a wide roasting tin and infuse the peeled garlic and the rest of the rosemary in it over a low heat on top of the stove.

- Remove the garlic with a slotted spoon and add the tomatoes. Pour in the half bottle of wine.

- Add the lamb shanks to the roasting tin, seal all over and place in the oven for an hour and a half. Pour the balsamic reduction over the lamb and continue to roast for a further 60 minutes or until tender.

- Remove the shanks to a large serving platter and place the oven tin on the stove over a medium heat, pour in the ½ glass of wine and stir, incorporating the juices in the tin. Pour this sauce over the shanks.

- Serve with chickpeas (*see recipe on page 209*) or chilli and garlic lentils (*see recipe on page 210*).

FILLET OF PORK WITH PORCINI AND TRUFFLE STUFFING, AND BALSAMIC REDUCTION

Filetto di maiale ripieno con funghi porcini e tartufo e riduzione balsamico

Piemontese pork, stuffed with porcini and truffle, is best eaten in front of a blazing log fire with a glass of Barbaresco!

INGREDIENTS – SERVES 4

2 fillets of organic pork
100g dried porcini mushrooms
200g dried breadcrumbs
50g freshly grated parmigiano
1 black truffle, grated, or truffle oil
Bunch of fresh parsley, finely chopped
2 cloves of garlic
1 organic egg yolk
1 eating apple, sliced wafer-thin
A couple of sprigs of fresh thyme
½ glass of dry white wine
½ lemon
2 tablespoons of milk
100ml balsamic reduction *(see recipe on page 83)*
Salt to taste

METHOD

- Preheat the oven to 180 degrees.
- Place the apple slices in a bowl of iced water with the lemon.
- Soak the porcini in a cup of tepid water and 2 tablespoons of milk at room temperature for 30 minutes.
- Remove all fat from the meat and with a sharp knife make an incision along the side of each fillet to create a pouch.

- Remove the porcini with a slotted spoon, drain the juice and keep aside.

- To make the stuffing shred the porcini and toss together with the breadcrumbs, parsley, parmigiano, egg yolk, salt and grated truffle or a couple of drops of truffle oil.

- Line the pouch with the stuffing and seal with a couple of toothpicks.

- Place a baking tray on the stove and warm the garlic and thyme in the oil.

- Remove the garlic and thyme and seal the fillet on both sides in the oil, add the wine and increase the heat for a minute to cook off the alcohol, then return to a low heat.

- Cover the tray with some tin foil and place in the oven for 25 minutes.

- Remove the foil, pour the porcini juices over the meat and continue roasting for another 10 minutes or until the meat is cooked.

- Leave to rest for 5 minutes before carving.

- Serve on a bed of wafer-thin apple slices (pat dry the slices first) and drizzle with balsamic reduction and truffled potatoes *(see recipe on page 207)*.

Suggestion: Grate a sweet eating apple into the balsamic reduction and cook for the last 10 minutes of the cooking time.

ROSEMARY GRILLED LAMB CUTLETS

Agnello scottadito

Scottadito means burn (the) finger and these cutlets are traditionally eaten as finger food. They are easy to prepare but simply delicious.

INGREDIENTS – SERVES 4

12 organic new-season lamb cutlets
1 large bunch of fresh rosemary
1 level teaspoon of chilli flakes
4 cloves of garlic, crushed
1 lemon, halved
6 tablespoons of extra virgin olive oil
6 tablespoons of balsamic vinegar
Salt and freshly ground pepper

METHOD

- Place some greaseproof paper over the cutlets and pound as thin as possible, remove excess fat and rub each cutlet all over with the lemon.
- Place the cutlets in a large bowl and marinate with the rest of the ingredients, cover and leave for 2 hours in the fridge.
- In batches of four proceed to cook the cutlets on a very hot griddle pan.
- Start by sealing on each side and turn over a couple of times until still slightly pink in the middle.
- Serve immediately with our pan-fried peppers *(see recipe on page 208)* or refried broccoli *(see recipe on page 207)*.

Suggestion: I have allowed three per person but everyone will want more!

FILLET OF ORGANIC IRISH BEEF WITH RED WINE REDUCTION, PARMIGIANO PETALS AND ROCKET

Filetto di manzo biologico irlandese con una riduzione di vino rosso, petali di parmigiano e rughetta

Fillet dies an instant death with overcooking, to the extent that most chefs refuse to serve 'well done'. This can be a bone of contention between the kitchen staff and the floor staff, who want to please the customer on all counts, but in the end the customer has to get what they ask for.

INGREDIENTS – SERVES 4

4 x 220g fillets of organic Irish beef
200g parmigiano shavings
Bunch of fresh rocket
4 tablespoons of extra virgin olive oil
150ml red wine reduction *(see recipe on page 83)*
Freshly ground black pepper and coarse salt
Extra virgin olive oil for dressing

METHOD

- Coat the fillets with salt, pepper and 4 tablespoons of oil. Place on a very hot griddle pan and seal on both sides. Turn over a couple of times until the beef is cooked rare or medium rare.

- Transfer the fillets to a warm plate, pour over the wine reduction and dress with the parmigiano shavings and rocket.

- Drizzle over some excellent extra virgin olive oil.

- Serve with red cabbage *(see recipe on page 206)*.

Suggestion: My son Seán cooks the best fillet I have ever tasted anywhere. He assures me that the secret to a good fillet is searing on an extremely hot griddle pan. He also adds Irish whiskey to the reduction, so maybe that's why it tastes so good!

TRIPE WITH TOMATO, MINT AND PECORINO

Trippa alla Romana

I have to admit that our attempts to convert our customers to this wonderful Roman dish have been largely unsuccessful. Originally served in family-run trattorie it now features on the menus of a lot of high-end restaurants in Italy.

INGREDIENTS – SERVES 4–6

600g ready-to-use tripe cut into small strips (ask your butcher to do this for you)

500ml tomato passata or 2 tins of plum tomatoes (mash the plum tomatoes with a fork before using)

200g freshly grated Pecorino Romano cheese

4 tablespoons of extra virgin olive oil

1 glass of dry white wine

Soffritto of 1 carrot, stick of celery and onion

Bunch of fresh mint, finely chopped

Salt and ground black pepper

METHOD

- In a wide, heavy-based saucepan sauté the soffritto and a little of the mint in the oil on a low heat for 5 minutes.

- Add the tripe and stir to absorb the juices of the pan.

- Pour in the wine and increase the heat momentarily to cook off the alcohol, then return to a low heat.

- Add the tomato, salt and pepper, cover and cook for 45 minutes or until the tripe is soft. Shake the pot occasionally.

- Mix the Pecorino Romano and the rest of the mint together and fold into the tripe 5 minutes before cooking is complete.

- Serve piping hot.

Suggestion: Serve small portions as antipasti.

Polenta

The best polenta or corn meal we have eaten was cooked by our dear friends the Garofalo family in a huge copper pot over an open wood fire way up in the Italian Alps. The cooking process took a couple of hours of laborious work which involved gradually adding the corn meal to simmering water and stirring continuously. The polenta absorbed a distinctive smoked flavour from the fire, and along with a rich tomato and sausage sauce was superb.

BASIC RECIPE FOR POLENTA

INGREDIENTS – SERVES 6–8

250g polenta flour
1½ litres of water

METHOD

- Bring a large saucepan of boiling water to simmer and gradually add the polenta a little at a time.
- Stir continuously to ensure that the polenta doesn't lump. This takes around 45 minutes to an hour depending on the quality of the flour. It's good to share the task of stirring.
- The polenta is ready when it easily comes away from the side of the saucepan.
- Pour onto a large wooden board and dress; see following recipes.

Suggestion: There are also good ready-to-use polentas available.

POLENTA WITH MUSHROOMS AND GORGONZOLA

Polenta con funghi e Gorgonzola

Stefano's favourite!

INGREDIENTS – SERVES 4

320g polenta (fresh or ready-to-use)
500g mixed forest mushrooms
400g Gorgonzola cheese
100g freshly grated Grana Trentino cheese
1 shallot, finely sliced
4 tablespoons of extra virgin olive oil
1 glass of dry white wine
Sprig of thyme
Salt and pepper to taste

METHOD

- Sweat the shallot and thyme in the oil until the shallot becomes translucent.
- Remove the thyme with a slotted spoon and add the mushrooms.
- Pour in the wine and increase the heat momentarily to cook off the alcohol, then return to a low heat.
- Simmer for 10 minutes until the sauce is reduced, then add salt and pepper to taste.
- Meanwhile prepare the polenta as per page 194 or according to the instructions on the packet and when ready pour onto a large serving plate.
- Cover the polenta with the mushroom sauce, crumble the Gorgonzola over it and sprinkle with Grana Trentino.

Suggestion: Try also with our chilli and garlic spinach (see recipe on page 204) and goat's cheese.

POLENTA WITH ITALIAN SAUSAGE AND PORK RIBS

Polenta con salsicce e spuntature

My daughter Aislinn's favourite. Mellow-tasting polenta calls for a hearty sauce.

INGREDIENTS – SERVES 4

320g polenta (fresh or ready-to-use)
500ml tomato passata or 2 tins of plum tomatoes
250g spare ribs (ask your butcher to cut them to 5cm pieces)
250g Italian sausage
200g freshly grated Grana Trentino cheese
4 ripe beef tomatoes, chopped
4 bay leaves
½ glass of red wine
6 tablespoons of extra virgin olive oil
Soffritto of 1 finely diced carrot, stick of celery and shallot
Salt and pepper to taste

METHOD

- Sauté the soffritto and bay leaves in the oil and add the ribs and sausage.
- Pour in the red wine and increase the heat momentarily to cook off the alcohol, then return to a low heat.
- Add the tomatoes, salt and pepper to taste, cover and cook for 90 minutes.
- Stir occasionally and add some warm water if it starts to dry.
- Meanwhile cook the polenta as per page 194 or according to the instructions on the packet.
- When the polenta is ready it should easily come away from the side of the saucepan.
- Pour into a large serving dish, pour over the sauce and sprinkle with freshly grated Grana Trentino.

Suggestion: Make a double quantity of polenta. Leave half of the batch aside to cool. The polenta will set and the following day you can bake it in the oven for a couple of minutes with tomato sauce and mozzarella.

Side dishes

I Contorni

There is so much talk about the Mediterranean diet and its benefits, yet there are many misconceptions about what the Mediterranean diet is. It is less what the Italians are eating today and more what they ate in the 1950s – people who worked the land and had little means, but were active and lived on a diet of brown bread and pasta, pulses and lots of fruit and vegetables. Cheese and meat were eaten rarely and wine was drunk daily as a nutritional drink. We now know that this was a healthy diet high in antioxidants. Nowadays the Italians eat mainly white pasta and bread, and although olive oil is the preferred fat from Liguria to Sicily, the northern cuisine is very much dependent on butter and cream. Italians do, however, continue to be generally health conscious and eat vast amounts of fruit, vegetables and pulses. Italy is fortunate, given its geographical positioning and climate, to offer its citizens a huge diversity of fruits and vegetables that burst forth with every season.

BRAISED ARTICHOKES
Carciofi alla romana

Roman cuisine largely consists of three distinctive cuisines: the *Quinto Quarto* (the fifth quarter, meaning offal) which is prevalent in the Testaccio area; the *Cucina Giudea* (Jewish cuisine) from the ghetto; and the *Cucina Campagnola* (country cuisine), referring to the cuisine of the Castelli and the countryside around Rome. Artichokes play a pivotal role in the Roman Jewish cuisine, and although there is a bit of work involved in preparing artichokes it's well worth the effort.

INGREDIENTS – SERVES 4

4 medium-sized fresh Romanesco
    artichokes
2 cloves of crushed garlic
Bunch of parsley, finely chopped
Bunch of mint, finely chopped
4 tablespoons of extra virgin olive oil
½ glass of dry white wine
½ glass of warm water
½ lemon
Salt to taste

METHOD
- Pound the garlic, parsley, mint and salt together and leave to rest.
- Take the artichokes and remove the tough outer leaves. You need to be mercenary – there is no use leaving tough bitter leaves that will ultimately ruin the dish. Scoop out the furry beards from the centre and with a sharp knife cut across the top of the artichoke, at least 2.5cm, and chop off the jagged edges. Cut and scrape the stalks to about 3cm.
- Rub each artichoke all over with the lemon. Start to open the leaves of the artichokes and stuff with the parsley and mint mixture.
- Warm the oil in a saucepan and place the artichokes head down. Sauté for a couple of minutes over a low heat, then add the wine and cook for another couple of minutes. Add the warm water, cover and cook over a low heat for 20 to 30 minutes until the artichokes are tender.
- Check from time to time and add a little extra warm water if they start to dry up.

Suggestion: If you prepare the artichokes before cooking then leave them in a bowl of cold water with chopped lemon to maintain the vibrant colour. Artichokes served warm are ideal companions to fish or meat, but served cold are wonderful antipasti.

BRAISED VEGETABLES
Verdure brasate

A meal on its own when served with a little cheese and toasted bread.

INGREDIENTS – SERVES 4
2 leeks, cleaned and finely sliced
1 aubergine, diced

1 bell pepper, thinly sliced
2 each of the following vegetables
 cleaned and cut into batons:
 carrots, celery sticks, parsnips,
 potatoes, sweet potatoes
8 cherry tomatoes, halved
A little marjoram
6 tablespoons of extra virgin olive oil

METHOD
- In a heavy-based saucepan sweat the
 leeks in the oil over a low heat for
 about 5 minutes.
- Add the tomatoes and cook for
 another 5 minutes. Then add the rest
 of the vegetables and marjoram, cover
 and cook over a very low heat for
 15 minutes. Shake the pot from time
 to time. Drizzle with a good olive oil
 before serving.

*Suggestion: Serve with roast meats and add
other seasonal vegetables of your choice.
This is also a good lunch option with some
warm focaccia.*

SPINACH WITH CREAM OF PARMIGIANO
Spinaci con crema di parmigiano

Although this is meant for four, I could
eat a kilo cooked this way by myself!

INGREDIENTS – SERVES 4
800g spinach, washed
4 tablespoons of extra virgin olive oil
 or a knob of butter

100g freshly grated parmigiano
Salt and pepper

METHOD

- Blanch the spinach in a large saucepan of boiling salted water for 1 minute and drain in a colander, but retain a little of the cooking liquid.

- Warm the oil or butter in a saucepan and add the spinach and a couple of spoons of the cooking liquid. Fold in the parmigiano and some freshly grated black pepper and cook for a further 2 minutes.

STRING BEANS WITH BALSAMIC DRESSING
Fagiolini con balsamico

These can be prepared in advance and served warm or cold.

INGREDIENTS – SERVES 4

400g fresh string beans, cleaned and
    ready to use
4 tablespoons of balsamic vinegar
4 tablespoons of extra virgin olive oil
Salt

METHOD

- Cook the string beans *al dente* in boiling salted water and drain. Toss in a bowl with the vinegar and oil.

Suggestion: String beans are especially good with quail eggs. Boil the quail eggs, cool, peel and slice in half and serve on top of the beans.

BRUSSEL SPROUTS WITH LEEKS, ROSEMARY AND SPECK
Cavoli di Bruxelles con porri, rosmarino e speck

A newcomer to the Italian Christmas menu, complemented with tasty speck.

INGREDIENTS – SERVES 4

400g fresh brussel sprouts, cleaned
2 leeks, cleaned and sliced
150g speck, thinly sliced
6 tablespoons of extra virgin olive oil
1 sprig of rosemary
Salt

METHOD

- Cook the sprouts in plenty of boiling salted water until soft, then drain.

- In a heavy-based saucepan sweat the leeks in the oil until they become translucent.

- Add the speck and rosemary and continue to cook for a couple of minutes.

- Slice the sprouts in half and add to the pan, stir and serve with roast meats.

CARROTS WITH CREAM OF PARMIGIANO
Carote con crema di parmigiano

A simple way to enrich carrots.

INGREDIENTS – SERVES 4

400g small carrots, cut into batons

1 leek, cleaned and finely sliced
50g freshly grated parmigiano
4 tablespoons of extra virgin olive oil
Knob of butter
Salt and ground black pepper

METHOD

- Cook the carrots *al dente* in boiling salted water and drain.

- Sauté the leek in the oil over a gentle heat until it becomes translucent, add the carrots and coat with the oil.

- Now fold in the parmigiano and butter and stir to form a cream. Serve with freshly ground black pepper.

CHILLI AND GARLIC SPINACH

Spinaci aglio, olio e peperoncino

Spinach cooked this way is also wonderful eaten hot on bruschetta.

INGREDIENTS – SERVES 4

800g spinach, washed
2 cloves of garlic, peeled
4 tablespoons of extra virgin olive oil
½ teaspoon of dried chilli flakes
Salt to taste

METHOD

- In a large saucepan warm the garlic and chilli in the oil, add the spinach, cover and cook for a couple of minutes, stir until the leaves wilt, and salt to taste.

COURGETTES WITH LEEKS, RAISINS AND PINE NUTS

Zucchine con porri, uvetta e pinoli

Another Sicilian plate influenced by its proximity to North Africa.

INGREDIENTS – SERVES 4

4 medium courgettes, organic if possible, washed and thinly sliced
2 leeks, washed and thinly sliced
150ml warm water
6 tablespoons of extra virgin olive oil
1 tablespoon of raisins
1 tablespoon of Mediterranean pine nuts
Salt and pepper to taste

METHOD

- Sauté the leeks in the oil on a gentle heat until they become translucent, stir in the courgettes and coat in the oil, pour in the warm water, cover and cook for 10 minutes.

- Meanwhile pan toast the pine nuts on a hot griddle pan for 2 to 3 minutes.

- Add the raisins and pine nuts to the courgettes along with salt and pepper and cook for a further 5 minutes.

MUSHROOMS WITH GARLIC AND PARSLEY

Funghi trifolati

Funghi trifolati can be used on

bruschetta, in pasta and risotto dishes and to dress polenta.

INGREDIENTS – SERVES 4
400g champignon mushrooms, cleaned
   and thinly sliced
4 tablespoons of white wine
6 tablespoons of extra virgin olive oil
2 cloves of garlic, peeled
Bunch of fresh parsley, finely chopped
Salt and pepper

METHOD
- Sauté the garlic in the oil on a gentle heat for 2 minutes, add the mushrooms, parsley and wine and stir. Cover and cook for 10 minutes. Add a little salt to taste and plenty of freshly ground black pepper.

Suggestion: A hint of chilli is also good with the mushrooms.

PEAS WITH LEEK, PANCETTA AND MINT
Piselli con porri, pancetta e menta

Fresh peas are special and don't require much dressing, whereas leek, pancetta and mint make frozen peas more interesting.

INGREDIENTS – SERVES 4
400g frozen or fresh peas
100g pancetta, diced
2 leeks, cleaned and sliced thinly
4 fresh mint leaves
4 tablespoons of extra virgin olive oil

METHOD

- Cook the peas in boiling salted water for 5 minutes and drain, but retain a cup of the cooking water.

- Sauté the leeks and mint in the oil over a gentle heat, add the pancetta and stir, but do not allow to brown, then add the peas and a couple of spoons of the pea water.

- Cover and cook over a low heat for 10 more minutes.

RED CABBAGE WITH TEROLDEGO WINE SAUCE

Cavolo rosso con salsa di vino Teroldego

One of the few interesting vegetables of the Alps, combined with local speck and red wine it transforms into a wonderful contorno.

INGREDIENTS – SERVES 4

½ red cabbage, cleaned and finely chopped
2 shallots, finely sliced
250ml Teroldego red wine
150ml speck or pancetta (optional)
150ml simmering water
4 tablespoons of extra virgin olive oil
Salt and pepper to taste

METHOD

- Gently sauté the shallots in the oil until they become translucent, add the speck or pancetta followed by the cabbage and stir to absorb the flavours of the pan.

- Pour in the wine and increase the heat momentarily to cook off the alcohol, return to a low heat, add salt and pepper to taste, cover with the simmering water and cook for 30 minutes. If it begins to dry out, pour in some more simmering water.

Suggestion: This is excellent with roasts and braised meats.

REFRIED BROCCOLI
Broccoli ripassati in padella

A quick and tasty antidote to hunger is pasta or vegetables dressed with 'Aglio, olio e peperoncino' – garlic, oil and chilli. This works really well here with broccoli.

INGREDIENTS – SERVES 4
400g fresh broccoli florets
2 cloves of garlic, crushed
1 level teaspoon of chilli flakes
6 tablespoons of extra virgin olive oil
Salt

METHOD
- Cook the broccoli *al dente* in boiling salted water and drain, but retain a cup of the cooking water. Sauté the garlic and chilli in the oil for a couple of minutes and add the broccoli and a half cup of broccoli water, cover and cook for 3 minutes.

Suggestion: Good with lamb cutlets scottadito.

TRUFFLED POTATOES
Patate con tartufo
A way to make a simple dish of mashed potatoes sophisticated.

INGREDIENTS – SERVES 4
500g floury potatoes
100g salted butter at room temperature
150ml warm milk
10g fresh truffle or 10 drops of truffle oil
Salt and freshly ground black pepper

METHOD
- Boil the potatoes in their jackets and when cooked remove the floury potato from the skin. In a saucepan warm the milk with a good knob of butter. Add the potatoes and mash to obtain a creamy consistency. Fold in some salt and pepper, truffle or truffle oil and serve.

ROSEMARY ROAST POTATOES
Patate arrosto con rosmarino

INGREDIENTS – SERVES 4–6
20 baby new potatoes, washed
4 cloves of garlic, unpeeled
100ml extra virgin olive oil
Large sprig of fresh rosemary
Salt

METHOD
- Preheat the oven to 250 degrees. Cut the potatoes in half. Place in a roasting tin along with the garlic cloves, fresh

rosemary and salt to taste. Pour in the oil and toss the potatoes until they are well coated.

- Bake in the hot oven for about 45 minutes.

Suggestion: A nice variation is to bake the potatoes with a handful of black olives.

PAN-FRIED PEPPERS
Peperonata

The smell of *peperoni* escaping through the windows of apartment blocks in the centre of Rome announces the arrival of summer.

INGREDIENTS – SERVES 4
4 medium bell peppers
4 shallots, finely sliced
4 basil leaves
4 tablespoons of balsamic vinegar
150ml tomato passata or 2 chopped
    beef tomatoes
4 tablespoons of extra virgin olive oil
Pinch of salt

METHOD
- Slice the peppers in half, remove the seeds and pulp, and cut into strips.
- Sauté the shallots in the oil until they soften, add the peppers and vinegar and increase the heat momentarily. Add the tomato, basil and a pinch of salt.
- Cover and cook over a low heat for 30 minutes.

LEGUMES

I Legumi

Legumes are known in Italy as *la carne dei poveri*, the poor man's meat. Legumes have featured prevalently in the regional *cucina povera* (peasant cuisine) for centuries. The economic boom in the 1960s resulted in vast emigration from the farming communities of the south to the industrial north. Like most immigrants, they suffered injustice and consequently shunned their traditions and customs. Legumes became unfashionable. Fortunately they have been rediscovered and now feature extensively on Italian menus.

We prepare various beans, lentils and chickpeas for our soups, salads and bruschetta. We also like to blitz them as a creamy basis for our main courses. Initially it seems like a lot of work compared to opening a tin but it's just a matter of routine. Steep the beans overnight, boil them the next morning while you are getting ready for work or preparing the children for school and you will have them ready for the evening dinner.

BORLOTTI OR CANNELLINI BEANS

Fagioli borlotti o cannellini

INGREDIENTS – SERVES 4–6
200g dried borlotti or cannellini beans
1 whole onion, carrot and stick of
   celery, peeled
1 sprig of fresh thyme
Salt and freshly ground pepper

METHOD
- Steep the beans in a saucepan of cold water overnight. Rinse and drain and place in a large saucepan along with the whole onion, carrot, stick of celery, salt, pepper and sprig of fresh thyme.
- Add cold water to cover them by 6cm. Bring to the boil and simmer for about 1 hour or so, depending on the quality or characteristic of the bean.
- With a slotted spoon remove the thyme, onion, carrot and celery. Drain the beans but retain the liquid if you intend to make soup.

Suggestion: These beans are very good eaten like this drizzled with excellent olive oil and a nice bruschetta. Use them to add to salads and soups or blitz to prepare a cream and use with main courses.

CHICKPEAS
Ceci

We use these chickpeas for our soups

and salads or you can blitz them in a
blender along with a couple of spoons
of the cooking broth to form a cream,
which is great with lamb.

INGREDIENTS – SERVES 4–6

200g dried chickpeas
1 whole onion, carrot and stick of
    celery, peeled
Salt and pepper to taste
Good sprig of fresh rosemary

METHOD

• Steep the chickpeas in plenty of cold
  water overnight. Rinse and drain and
  place in a large saucepan along with
  the rosemary, whole carrot, stick of
  celery, onion, salt and pepper. Add
  cold water to cover by 6cm. Bring to
  the boil and simmer for about 1 hour
  or until soft. With a slotted spoon
  remove the onion, carrot and celery.
  Drain but retain the cooking liquid if
  you want to make chickpea soup.

CHILLI AND GARLIC LENTILS
Lenticchie stile marchigiana

Prepare these lentils to accompany
rabbit, fish or chicken dishes.

INGREDIENTS – SERVES 4–6

320g Castelluccio lentils
1 shallot, carrot and stick of celery
1 ripe beef tomato, chopped
1 teaspoon of chilli flakes
½ glass of red wine

2 cloves of garlic, peeled
6 tablespoons of extra virgin olive oil
1 sprig of thyme
1 tablespoon of salt

METHOD

• Rinse the lentils several times to
  remove any grit and place in a
  saucepan of 1½ litres of cold water,
  along with the shallot, carrot and
  celery and 1 tablespoon of salt.

• Cover and bring to the boil and
  then simmer for 40 minutes or until
  the lentils are cooked. They should
  have absorbed most of the liquid but
  remained moist. If they dry up during
  the cooking add some hot water – it
  will depend on the quality of the lentil.
  Some lentils require more cooking
  time than others: it can range from 40
  minutes to an hour and 15 minutes.

• Remove the shallot, carrot and celery
  from the pot with a slotted spoon.
  Sauté the garlic, chilli and thyme in the
  oil over a gentle heat, stir in the lentils
  and mix, pour in the wine and increase
  the heat momentarily to cook off the
  alcohol, then return to a low heat. Add
  the chopped tomato, cover and cook
  for a further 5 minutes.

CREAM OF BROAD BEANS WITH CHILLI OIL
Crema di fave con olio di peperoncino

The first of May, *il primo maggio* or il
giorno dei lavoratori (workers' day), is a

public holiday and is celebrated with fresh broad beans and chunks of fresh Roman Pecorino cheese. Piles of broad bean pods are placed in the middle of the table with chunks of Pecorino, and everyone hacks away at the cheese and shells the beans, discarding the pods indiscriminately.

INGREDIENTS – SERVES 4–6

400g fresh broad beans, shelled
1 whole onion, carrot and stick of celery
1 tablespoon of dried marjoram
5 tablespoons of extra virgin olive oil
1 level tablespoon of chilli flakes
2 cloves of garlic, peeled
Salt to taste

METHOD

- Place the broad beans, onion, carrot, celery, salt and marjoram in a sauce-pan and cover with cold water. Bring to the boil, then simmer for 10 minutes or until the broad beans are tender. Remove the carrot, celery and onion with a slotted spoon and drain the broad beans, but retain the cooking liquid. Place the broad beans in a blender with 1 tablespoon of oil and 1 clove of garlic and blitz to obtain a creamy consistency. If it's too dry add some of the cooking liquid to moisten.

- Meanwhile pound the rest of the oil, the other clove of garlic and chilli flakes together. Pour the broad bean cream into a bowl and drizzle with the chilli oil.

Desserts

I Dolci

Religious festivals are always associated with speciality foods. Easter time in Naples centres around the famous *Pastiera* cake. People talk about nothing else for weeks beforehand – where to buy the best ricotta, for how long the *grana* should be steeped in rosewater – and each family guards its own secret recipe of course. *La Cassata di Sant'Agata*, a Sicilian Easter treat, is an almond paste and ricotta dessert that resembles the breasts of the Saint Agata. *Colomba*, a sponge cake with almond icing in the shape of a dove, is eaten throughout Italy at Easter (introduced in the 1930s by Motta, the company behind a large portion of commercialised *panettone* and *pandoro* cakes; most Italians nowadays think it always existed!), while *panettone* and *pandoro*, sponge cakes, are traditionally eaten at Christmas. The desserts we serve at Dunne & Crescenzi are everyday desserts but nonetheless special because of the addition of those precious drops of *vinsanto* or *limoncello* or fresh ricotta from Siena.

TIRAMISÙ WITH VINSANTO

Tiramisù al vinsanto

When we ran our little deli in Sutton back in 1995, neighbours would often ask us to cater for family gatherings, pre-wedding dinners, etc. Tiramisù was particularly popular – a combination of chocolate, cream cheese and coffee that most people adore. We have tried various liquors but find that vinsanto gives it an elegant lift.

INGREDIENTS – SERVES 6

350g mascarpone
60g castor sugar
250g packet of savoiardi biscuits
2 organic or free-range eggs
1 teaspoon of granulated sugar
½ glass of Tuscan vinsanto dessert
 wine

1 glass of cold black coffee (avoid
 instant coffee: instead use a very
 long espresso)
4 tablespoons of unsweetened dark
 chocolate cocoa powder, at least
 60%

METHOD

- Separate the whites and the yolks of the eggs. Whisk the whites until stiff and set aside, cream the mascarpone, yolks and castor sugar, and gently fold in the beaten egg whites.

- Sweeten the coffee with 1 teaspoon of granulated sugar and the vinsanto liquor. Pour into a bowl and dip the savoiardi biscuits one by one into the coffee – this should be done briskly, to avoid the biscuits becoming soggy.

- Coat the bottom of a baking dish with a layer of the mascarpone cream followed by a layer of savoiardi, and alternate until all of the ingredients are consumed, finishing with a layer of the cream.

- Cover with cling film and refrigerate for at least 2 hours. Sprinkle with the dark cocoa powder just before serving.

Suggestion: The tiramisù should only be coated with the dark cocoa powder just before serving, otherwise it will soak into the cream and appear dull and uninteresting.

RICOTTA AND AMARENE CHERRY TART

Torta di ricotta e amarene

INGREDIENTS – SERVES 6–8

Ricotta filling
600g fresh ricotta cheese
300g granulated sugar
4 organic or free-range eggs
Grated rind of 1 lemon
Grated rind of 1 orange
Pinch of cinnamon
1 espresso cup of brandy
1 can of amarene cherries in syrup,
   drained

Pastry
200g plain flour
50g finely ground almonds
95g unsalted butter at room
   temperature, cut into cubes
95g granulated sugar
2 organic or free-range eggs
1 beaten egg yolk for glazing
Pinch of salt

METHOD

- *For the filling:* Separate the egg yolks from the whites, whisk the whites until stiff and beat the yolks. Toss all of the ingredients except the egg whites together. Fold in the egg whites and leave aside; in this way the ricotta soaks up the flavours (actually this is extremely good to eat as is).

- *For the pastry:* Mix the dry ingredients in a bowl and turn onto a floured board. Make a well and put the eggs and butter in the middle. Work the flour in from the edges toward the centre with your fingers, incorporating all of the ingredients. Knead lightly and quickly to form a soft dough. Wrap the pastry in greaseproof paper and leave to rest in the fridge for at least an hour.

- Roll out the pastry to line a greased 25cm spring-form baking tin and blind bake as follows: line the base of the tin with pastry, prick with a fork in several places and place in the fridge for 20 minutes or so.

- Preheat the oven to 180 degrees. Remove the pastry from the fridge, cover with grease-proof paper and place some rice or dried beans or lentils on top. Bake for 10 minutes.

- Glaze the pastry with some egg yolk and spread the ricotta mixture over the top. Bake in the oven for about 30 minutes or until the pastry takes on a gorgeous golden colour. Serve warm or cool.

  Suggestion: You can substitute amarene cherries with broken dark chocolate, if you prefer.

RICH CHOCOLATE CAKE FROM CAPRI

Torta Caprese

Pastry shops do most of their weekly business on Sundays. From early morning they are busy fulfilling orders. Golden cardboard trays of various sizes are filled with dainty pastries and packaged in pretty paper and bows. Large cakes are boxed and tied with colourful ribbons. Families enjoy long lingering lunches on Sundays, and someone is designated to collect the *dolci*. This is a Sunday treat from the island of Capri.

INGREDIENTS – SERVES 6

250g unsalted butter
250g dark chocolate 60%
300g coarse-ground almonds
200g granulated sugar
5 organic or free-range eggs

METHOD

- Preheat the oven to 180 degrees.
- Separate the whites from the egg yolks.
- Whip the egg whites until stiff and beat the egg yolks.
- Snap the chocolate into small pieces, place in a bowl and melt in an improvised bain-marie (i.e. place the bowl over a saucepan of simmering water).
- Meanwhile cream the butter and sugar and then stir in the beaten egg yolks.
- Incorporate the chocolate and almonds followed by the beaten egg whites.
- Place the mixture in a greased 22cm spring-form cake tin and cook for 1 hour at 180 degrees.

Suggestion: Serve moist and warm with a scoop of vanilla ice cream.

LIMONCELLO AND PEACH CAKE

Torta con le pesche e limoncello

We introduced this cake to the restaurant after a memorable trip to Furore on the Amalfi coast, to evoke the unforgettable lemon aromas that continue to haunt visitors for years after.

INGREDIENTS – SERVES 6

150g self-raising flour
150g granulated sugar
200g butter
100g fresh cream
3 organic or free-range eggs
½ teaspoon of lemon zest
4 small ready-to-eat peaches, peeled and sliced thick
4 tablespoons of limoncello liquor

METHOD

- Preheat the oven to 180 degrees.
- Melt the butter.
- Beat the eggs with the sugar into a syrup in a bowl and add the sieved flour, warm butter, cream and lemon zest and mix gently.
- Pour the mixture into a greased 23cm oven dish and place the slices of peach on top.
- Bake at 180 degrees for 35 minutes or until a skewer comes out clean.
- Drizzle with limoncello while the cake is still very hot.
- Leave to cool a little on a wire rack, but it is best served warm (it doesn't keep well).

Suggestion: Serve with a good vanilla ice cream.

PANNACOTTA WITH FRUITS OF THE FOREST

Pannacotta con frutti di bosco

Pannacotta, cooked cream, is a versatile dessert which lends itself to various sauces from chocolate to forest fruits.

INGREDIENTS – SERVES 4

1 litre of double cream	100g blackberries
2 vanilla pods	100g strawberries
3 gelatine leaves	100g raspberries
150ml milk	1¼ teaspoon of lemon zest
150g icing sugar	1 tablespoon of granulated sugar

METHOD

- *For the pannacotta:* Soak the gelatine in the milk for 10 minutes. Remove the gelatine, warm the milk until simmering, then stir the gelatine back into the milk and dissolve.

- Meanwhile heat the cream along with the icing sugar, until it simmers. Slice the vanilla pods lengthways and scrape the seeds into the cream, then simmer until it reduces by a third. Pass the milk through a strainer into the cream mixture, stir gently and leave to cool. Pour the pannacotta mixture into four 200ml ramekins, cover with tinfoil and leave to set in the fridge for at least 20 hours.

- *For the fruits of the forest syrup:* Place all of the fruits, the granulated sugar, lemon zest and 2 tablespoons of cold water in a heavy-based saucepan and cook over a low heat for 10 minutes.

- Leave aside to cool. You can strain the juice from the fruit if you prefer, but we serve the cooked fruits at the restaurant.

- Turn out each pannacotta onto a tea plate and serve with the fruit and syrup.

Suggestion: For another interesting pannacotta, pannacotta con nocciole (pannacotta with crushed nuts), simply add a tablespoon of quality hazelnut or chocolate spread into the cream while simmering. Sprinkle with crushed pistachio or hazelnuts before serving.

DARK CHOCOLATE, PEAR AND RICOTTA CAKE

Torta di ricotta, pera e cioccolata

INGREDIENTS – SERVES 6–8

A batch of pastry *(see recipe on page 217)*
600g fresh ricotta cheese
300g granulated sugar
250g quality dark chocolate
4 organic or free-range eggs
4 mature pears
Grated rind of 1 orange
Pinch of cinnamon
1 espresso cup of brandy

METHOD

- *For the filling:* Preheat the oven to 180 degrees. Separate the egg yolks from the whites, whisk the whites until stiff and beat the yolks. In a mixing bowl gently stir the ricotta, egg yolks, 200g of the sugar, orange rind, brandy and cinnamon. Now fold in the egg whites and leave aside for 5 minutes.

- Peel the pears and cut into slices of 2cm. Place the pears in a small saucepan along with 100g of sugar and 50ml of water. Cover and simmer over a low heat for about 10 minutes until the pears are soft.

- Melt the chocolate bain-marie style.

- Roll out the pastry to line a greased 25cm spring-form baking tin and blind bake as in the recipe for ricotta and cherry tart *(see recipe on page 217)*.

- Paint a layer of melted chocolate over the pastry base and cover this with a layer of pears, then spread the ricotta mixture over the top.

- Simply swirl in the rest of the melted chocolate or for a more dramatic look pipe a line of chocolate across the cake and with the tip of a knife drag the chocolate outwards from centre to create an interesting design.

- Bake in the oven for 30 minutes. Serve at room temperature.

CIAMBELLONE YOGHURT SPONGE CAKE

Ciambellone allo yogurt

Ciambellone is a circular sponge cake and olive oil is used instead of butter. It can be kept for up to a week. Serve fresh for breakfast or afternoon tea, and when it starts to dry serve for dunking in coffee or wine.

INGREDIENTS – SERVES 6

200g granulated sugar
120g natural yoghurt
200g plain all-purpose flour
4 organic or free-range eggs
1 espresso cup of extra virgin olive oil
½ cup of milk
1 level teaspoon of baking powder
Grated rind of 1 lemon

METHOD

- Preheat the oven to 180 degrees.
- Cream the eggs and sugar together and then fold in the yoghurt, oil, lemon rind and milk.
- Sieve the flour and baking powder into the mixture and stir.
- Pour into a greased 22cm spring-form savarin circular mould and bake for around 40 minutes or until a skewer comes out clean.

Suggestion: Add cocoa powder to half of the mixture and the family can choose between plain or chocolate.

SHORTCAKE JAM TART

Crostata alla marmellata

Outside school gates Italian mothers regularly discuss the importance of *una merenda genuina* (a genuine snack) for their children. Often they take turns to bake for the whole class to ensure that the snacks are natural. The most popular are jam tarts and ciambellone.

INGREDIENTS – SERVES 6

200g plain all-purpose flour
150g granulated sugar
150g butter
1 organic or free-range egg, beaten
1 egg yolk, beaten for glazing the pastry
Pinch of salt
½ teaspoon of lemon zest
1 jar of strawberry, raspberry or apricot jam

METHOD

- Preheat the oven to 180 degrees.
- Add the butter to the flour and crumble, form a well in the middle of the mixture and add the sugar, salt, lemon zest and beaten free-range egg, and start to mix with your fingers until a soft dough is formed. Wrap in greaseproof paper and leave in the fridge for an hour or so.
- Remove the pastry from the fridge and when it is at room temperature divide it into two, one section being fifty per cent larger than the other. Roll out the larger section to line a 23cm greased pie tin.
- Spread the jam over the pastry. Take the second pastry section, roll it out and cut into long 2cm-wide strips. Lay the strips over the tart to create a lattice effect, seal the edges with beaten egg yolk and glaze the pastry with some more beaten egg. Cook in the oven for 20 to 30 minutes.
- Serve with freshly whipped cream.

CANTUCCINI BISCUITS

Biscotti Cantuccini

Many Italian biscuits are cooked twice, hence the name biscotti – *bis* (twice) *cotti* (cooked). The first baking is to cook the biscuits and the second baking is to dry and therefore preserve them.

INGREDIENTS FOR 30 BISCUITS

200g plain all-purpose flour
150g castor sugar
1 level teaspoon of baking powder
2 organic or free-range eggs, beaten

100g blanched almonds
50g coarse-ground almonds
½ teaspoon of orange zest

METHOD

- Preheat the oven to 150 degrees.
- Pan toast the blanched almonds very quickly on a hot skillet.
- Mix the flour, baking powder, sugar and ground almonds together and moisten with the beaten eggs.
- Add the blanched almonds and orange zest and knead to form a soft dough.
- Roll the dough into a thick log and cut in half to form two logs about 5cm in diameter and 30cm long. Bake on a greased tin for around 20 minutes.
- Remove and cool on a wire rack. Then slice into biscuits at 2cm intervals and return to the oven for another 15 minutes.
- Spread out on a rack to cool before storing in an airtight container.

Suggestion: Serve with an aged vinsanto dessert wine – the biscuits can be dunked in the vinsanto as a pleasant dessert alternative.

CAT'S TONGUE BISCUITS

Biscotti lingue di gatto

INGREDIENTS FOR ABOUT 24 BISCUITS

100g butter at room temperature
100g castor sugar
100g plain flour

½ teaspoon of lemon zest
2 egg whites

METHOD

- Preheat the oven to 180 degrees.

- Whisk the egg whites until stiff. Cream the butter and sugar together and incorporate the egg whites and lemon zest.

- Sieve in the flour and mix gently. Spoon the mixture into an icing pouch with a 1cm nozzle. Pipe lines of about 10cm placed well apart onto a greased baking tray.

- Bake in the oven for 5 minutes until the tongues take on a golden colour.

LEMON ALMOND BISCUITS

Amaretti al limone

INGREDIENTS FOR ABOUT 24 BISCUITS

250g ground almonds
250g icing sugar
1 teaspoon of lemon juice

3 egg whites
1 teaspoon of lemon zest

METHOD

- Preheat the oven to 180 degrees.

- In a mixing bowl whisk the egg whites until stiff. Toss the dry ingredients and lemon zest together and gradually fold in the egg whites and lemon juice.

- Take a teaspoon and spoon dollops of the mixture well spaced out onto a greased oven tray, and bake for 10 minutes.

- Remove from the oven and cool on a wire rack.

DUNNE & CRESCENZI CHEESE BOARD

I Formaggi

Stefano adores cheese and when we work late he quickly puts together a cheese-board, tosses a salad and treats us to a glass of Amarone. Cheese boards are a lovely way to end a meal as they're about sharing and everyone helping themselves. Arrange an interesting selection of cheeses on a large board – mature cheeses like Parmigiano Reggiano from Emilia or Grana from Trentino and Pecorino sheep's cheese from Tuscany, along with some semi-soft cheeses like Fontina from Alto Adige and Taleggio from Lombardy and some smoked Provola from Campania. Serve with wild honey and toasted focaccia. We like to feature excellent Irish cheeses on the menu such as Cashel Blue from Tipperary, Gubbeen from West Cork and Coolea, also from Cork.

Coffee

Italian bars are in reality coffee bars, and the buzz in the morning is fantastic, with people of all ages and backgrounds coming and going, standing at the bar (where breakfasts are generally consumed), pushing and shoving in desperation to get the attention of the *barista* (bar tender). Amidst the chaos it is not unusual to observe smartly dressed executives dunk large *cornetti* (croissants) into tiny espresso cups (for Italians are fond of dunking).

Italy has cultivated a serious coffee culture for centuries that has given rise to a breed of master blenders and roasters. A huge amount of secrecy, akin to a secret sect, surrounds their skills and knowledge. Recently we met with owners of established coffee houses who run the risk of going out of business because their children are not interested in taking over the family business, but still the owners refuse to divulge their knowledge to 'outsiders'.

There is an art to making good coffee. The two main varieties of coffee are *Arabica* and *Robusta*. *Arabica* is the more prestigious and produces a mellow and aromatic coffee. *Robusta* on the other hand is bitter, woody, higher in caffeine, foams better than *Arabica* and provides depth and cream. Successful coffee blends are usually made up of a high percentage of fragrant *Arabica* with a touch of *Robusta*. Italian *baristi* spend years training in the art of coffee-making, understanding the *miscela* (coffee blends), maintaining the machinery and building relationships with customers. The *barista* is responsible for making coffee, cocktails, sodas and so on, and is considered a respected professional. When we travel to Rome and visit our favourite cafés, it is pleasant to be greeted and remembered by the *baristi* who have been there for the last thirty years.

When you travel throughout Italy you should not ask for a *latte*, unless you want a glass of milk, you should ask for a *caffè latte*. Expect to be treated with contempt should you ask for a *cappuccino* or *caffè latte* after 11 a.m. as milk-based coffees are only drunk in the morning. For a simple black coffee ask for an *Americano* (a throwback to the arrival of American troops in Naples towards the end of the Second World War and their preference for black coffee). A request for *un caffè* means an *espresso* and most meals finish with an *espresso* or an *espresso corretto* (with the addition of a liquor such as *sambuca*, *averna* or *amaro*). In Rome *ammazza caffè* (kill the coffee) is popular and consists of an *espresso* followed by a shot of liquor, the concept being that the liquor should counterbalance the caffeine in the coffee.

Wine

Il vino

Italy has the greatest variety of grapes in the world, numbering around 3,000, and around 400 are cultivated. Nowadays there is an emphasis on reviving the cultivation of indigenous grapes as part of the local and slow-food ideology, i.e. to preserve species and encourage biodiversity, protect valid food-production techniques and promote ethical production in general. When we travel throughout Italy, it can be the little defects of a wine that characterise it and make it special. And while a Langhe Nebbiolo from Gaja in Piedmont is sublime, at the same time Marisa Cuomo's Fiorduva from Furore on the Amalfi Coast is unforgettable and great in its own right.

The Dunne & Crescenzi wine list of over 200 labels intends to be representative of the great variety of wine producers from various regions of Italy. A number of the producers who appear on the list were chosen because, having met them, we wanted to support their passion for what they are doing.

Filippo Antonelli, who produces one of the best Sagrantinos in Montefalco (Umbria), is so passion-

ate about what he is doing that he sacrificed a successful legal career to dedicate himself full-time to his vineyard. Filippo once told me, 'I abandoned a family business of four generations to dedicate time to my vineyard and now my wallet is half empty but my soul is content.' He has recently started a vineyard in Lazio and I am sure we can expect extraordinary things from there in a couple of years' time.

Marisa Cuomo is an amazing woman who, along with her husband, cultivates a vineyard beaten into the side of the rocks high above the Amalfi coast. The cultivation is hard and labour intensive and their lives are written on their hands.

Elizabetta Foradori from Trentino is another extraordinary woman dedicated to biodynamic cultivation who has taken the Teroldego grape variety to a new level.

Casale del Giglio and Principe Pallavacini are delivering wonderful wines from Lazio, which hitherto was synonymous with nasty Frascati.

A number of co-operatives are producing very good wines and we represent the wines from Cormons in Friuli on our wine list.

When we meet Giuseppe Soini from Cormons he talks as eagerly about a neighbour who produces the greatest Prosciutto San Daniele as about his wines. Roberto Bava's Barbera d'Asti is extraordinary, but he continually sends us tastings of local cheese, chocolate and truffles. Italy is full of passionate producers who are proud of what they produce and are eager to pass on their skills to the next generation, and more importantly they act as ambassadors for their local areas and regions.

Wine Suggestions

In suggesting wines to pair with food we decided in some cases to suggest a sparkling wine, a white or a red wine or indeed white and red. This emanates from our experience on the restaurant floor. A number of our patrons may only drink white or only red and we believe it to be a matter of personal choice. We write daily specials on our boards in the restaurant and suggest wines to go with each dish. The boards are called *Si consiglia* (it is suggested): *Un vino frizzante* recommends a sparkling wine, *Un vino bianco* recommends a white wine and *Un vino rosso* recommends a red wine. We both enjoy Prosecco with antipasti, while Stefano has a preference for rosé wines and northern whites, and I love big bold reds. The majority of white wines should be drunk young, preferably no more than two years old. Here are some suggestions taken from our wine list to compliment the recipes.

ANTIPASTI

GRILLED MEDITERRANEAN VEGETABLES: *White wine/Un vino bianco:* Frascati Superior, Poggio Verde '09, Principe Pallavicini (Lazio). *Red wine/Un vino rosso:* Marzemino Trentino '10 Doc, Istituto Agrario S. Michele all'Adige (Trentino).

CAMPANIA BUFFALO MOZZARELLA, AUBERGINE AND PRAWN STACK: *White wine/Un vino bianco:* Greco di Tufo '09 Docg, Feudi di San Gregorio (Campania).

BRESAOLA FROM VALTELLINA, RUCOLA AND PARMIGIANO: *Sparkling wine/Un vino frizzante:* Franciacorta Extra Brut Riserva '04, La Montina (Lombardy). *Red wine/Un vino rosso:* Valtellina Superiore '08, Dirupi (Lombardy).

PORTOBELLO MUSHROOMS WITH GORGONZOLA AND PESTO STUFFING: *Sparkling wine/Un vino frizzante:* Prosecco Cartizze Superiore Valdobbiadene Docg, Astoria (Veneto). *White wine/Un vino bianco:* Muller Thurgau '09 Doc, Abbazia di Novacella (Alto Adige). *Red wine/Un vino rosso:* S. Magdalener '09 Doc, Abbazia di Novacella (Alto Adige).

SMOKED IRISH SALMON WITH AVOCADO, GOAT'S CHEESE AND ROCKET: *Sparkling wine/Un vino frizzante:* Prosecco Millesimato Valdobbiadene '09 Docg, Astoria (Veneto). *White wine/Un vino bianco:* Nosiola Trentino '09 Doc, Istituto Agrario S. Michele all'Adige (Trentino). *Rosé/Un vino rosé:* Rosander Pinot Grigio '09, Cormons (Friuli).

CAMPANIA BUFFALO MOZZARELLA WITH GRILLED PEPPERS AND FRESH BASIL. *White wine/Un vino bianco:* Greco di Tufo '09 Docg, Feudi di San Gregorio (Campania). *Red wine/Un vino rosso:* Serpico '04, Feudi di San Gregorio (Campania).

PROSCIUTTO SAN DANIELE WITH BABY SPINACH, GRANA TRENTINO CHEESE SHAVINGS AND RADICCHIO: *White wine/Un vino bianco:* Chardonnay Collio '09 Doc, Cormons (Friuli). *Red wine/Un vino rosso:* Pinot Nero '07, Maculan (Veneto).

SAUTÉ OF MUSSELS: *White wine/Un vino bianco:* Tinaia bianco Salento, Salento '09, Cantine Due Palme (Puglia). *Rosé/Un vino rosé:* Rosato Due Palme '09, Cantine Due Palme (Puglia).

SPECK AND ASIAGO POLENTA CROSTINI: *White wine/Un vino bianco:* Valle Isarco Sulvaner '09, Abbazia di Novacella (Alto Adige). *Red wine/Un vino rosso:* S. Magdalener '09 Doc, Abbazia di Novacella (Alto Adige).

POLENTA AND SPINACH CROSTINI: *White wine/Un vino bianco:* Muller Thurgau '10 Doc, Abbazia del Novacella (Alto Adige). *Red wine/Un vino rosso:* Marzemino Trentino '10 Doc, Istituto Agrario S. Michele all'Adige (Trentino).

238

BRUSCHETTA WITH FRESH VINE-RIPENED TOMATOES AND BASIL: *White wine/Un vino bianco:* Pecorino '08, Luigi Cataldi Madonna (Abruzzo). *Red wine/Un vino rosso:* Tatone Montepulciano d'Abruzzo '07 Doc, Terra d'Aligi (Abruzzo).

BRUSCHETTA WITH MUSHROOMS AND RICOTTA BOWS: *White wine/Un vino bianco:* Falanghina Doc, Feudi di San Gregorio (Campania). *Red wine/Un vino rosso:* Nero d'Avola '09, Antonini Ceresa (Sicily).

BRUSCHETTA WITH TUNA, OLIVES, CAPERS AND SUN-DRIED TOMATOES: *White wine/Un vino bianco:* Chardonnay '08, Planeta (Sicily). *Red wine/Un vino rosso:* Merlot '09 Doc, Erice (Sicily).

BRUSCHETTA WITH BORLOTTI BEANS AND TOMATO: *White wine/Un vino bianco:* Gavi di Gavi, Cor di Chasse '09, Bava (Piedmont). *Red wine/Un vino rosso:* Nobile di Montepulciano Riserva '06, Bindella (Tuscany).

BAKED CROSTINI WITH ANCHOVIES, PROSCIUTTO DI PARMA, TOMATO, PARMIGIANO AND ROCKET: *White wine/Un vino bianco:* Ferrata '09, Maculan (Veneto). *Red wine/Un vino rosso:* Valdadige Schiava '09 Doc, Istituto Agrario S. Michele all'Adige (Trentino).

SOUPS

MINESTRONE SOUP: *White wine/Un vino bianco:* Poggio Verde, Frascati Superiore '09, Principe di Pallavicini (Lazio). *Red wine/Un vino rosso:* Cesanese '09, Principe di Pallavicini (Lazio).

BORLOTTI BEAN SOUP: *Red wine/Un vino rosso:* Tatone Montepulciano d'Abruzzo '07, Terra d'Aligi (Abruzzo).

BUTTERNUT SQUASH, SCALLOP AND ALMOND SOUP: *White wine/Un vino bianco:* Chardonnay Collio '09 Doc, Cormons (Friuli).

CHICKPEA SOUP WITH PASTA: *White wine/Un vino bianco:* Lacryma Chrisi Doc, Feudi di San Gregorio (Campania). *Red wine/Un vino rosso:* Tatone Montepulciano d'Abruzzo '07, Terra d'Aligi (Abruzzo).

LENTIL AND MUSSEL SOUP: *White wine/Un vino bianco:* Verdicchio di Castelli di Jesi Superiore, Serra Vecchie vigne '08, Umani Ronchi (Marche). *Red wine/Un vino rosso:* Rosso Conero '08, Malacari (Marche).

PEA, PRAWN AND MINT SOUP: *White wine/Un vino bianco:* Falanghina 2001 Fontanavecchia (Campania). *Red wine/Un vino rosso:* Montevetrano 2007 (Campania).

SALADS

Gaeta olive salad: *White wine/Un vino bianco:* Greco di Tufo '09 Docg, Feudi di San Gregorio (Campania). *Rosé/Un vino rosé:* Albiola '09, Casale del Giglio (Lazio).

Warm chicken salad with pancetta and peppers: *White wine/Un vino bianco:* Sitrico '09, Casale del Giglio (Lazio). *Rosé/Un vino rosé:* Albiola '09, Casale del Giglio (Lazio).

Warm goat's cheese salad with William pear and walnuts: *Sparkling wine/Un vino frizzante:* Prosecco Valdobbiadene, Astoria (Veneto). *White wine/Un vino bianco:* Pinot Grigio '09, Cormons (Friuli). *Red wine/Un vino rosso:* Terresicci Isola di Nuragi '09, Cantine di Dolianova (Sardinia).

Orange and fennel salad: *White wine/Un vino bianco:* Chardonnay Contessa Entellina la Fuga '09, Donnafugata (Siciliy). *Rosé/Un vino rosé:* Nero d'Avola '09, Feudo Maccari (Sicily).

Puntarelle with anchovy sauce: *Red wine/Un vino rosso:* Syrah '09, Principe di Pallavicini (Lazio). *White wine/Un vino bianco:* Orvieto '09, Sergio Mottura (Lazio).

Marche Bomba salad: *Red wine/Un vino rosso:* Piancarda Rosso Concero '09, Garofoli (Marche). *White wine/Un vino bianco:* Offida Pecorino '09, Fiorano (Marche).

PASTA

Ravioli with ricotta and spinach:*White wine/Un vino bianco:* Earth Heart '09, Leone Conti (Emilia Romagna).

Ravioli with smoked Irish salmon and orange zest: *Un vino frizzante rosé:* Pinto Nero brut metodo classico VSQ millesimo, Cocchi (Piedmont). *White wine/Un vino bianco:* Lugana Doc, Bertani (Veneto).

Spinach and ricotta tortelli with parmigiano cream and balsamic reduction: *White wine/Un vino bianco:* Gavi di Gavi, Cor de Chasse '09, Bava (Piedmont). *Red wine/Un vino rosso:* Refosco Aqileian '09 Doc, Cormons (Friuli).

Dunne & Crescenzi pasta with tomato and basil sauce: *White wine/Un vino bianco:* Bertesca Vernaccia di San Gimignano '09 Docg, Castelli del Grevepesa (Tuscany). *Red wine/Un vino rosso:* Pontorno '09, Chianti Classico, Castelli del Grevepesa (Tuscany).

SQUID INK PASTA WITH FRUITS OF THE SEA: *White wine/Un vino bianco:* Costa d'Amalfi, Fiorduva '09, Marisa Cuomo, Furore (Campania). *Rosé/Un vino rosé:* Costa d'Amalfi rosato '09, Marisa Cuomo, Furore (Campania).

STROZZAPRETI WITH AUBERGINES, PINE NUTS, SPECK AND CHERRY TOMATOES:*White wine/Un vino bianco:* Greco di bianco '08, Stelitano (Calabria). *Red wine/Un vino rosso:* Organic Ciro' rosso superior a vita '08, Vigna de Franco (Calabria).

FETTUCCINE WITH SALMON AND COURGETTE: *Sparkling wine/Un vino frizzante:* Prosecco, Cartizze Superiore Valdobbiadene Docg, Astoria (Veneto): *White wine/Un vino bianco:* Lucana '09 Doc, Bertani (Veneto). *Red wine/Un vino rosso:* Baiocco '09, Antonelli (Umbria).

BUCATINI PASTA WITH GUANCIALE AND TOMATO: *White wine/Un vino bianco:* Pecorino '09, Terra d'Aligi (Abruzzo). *Red wine/Un vino rosso:* Montepulciano d'Abruzzo Tolos '07 Docg, Terra d'Aligi (Abruzzo).

PACCHERI PASTA FROM GRAGNANO WITH DUBLIN BAY PRAWNS AND TOMATO: *White wine/Un vino bianco:* Tinaia Bianco Salento, Salento '09, Cantine Due Palme (Puglia). *Rosé/Un vino rosé:* Rosato Due Palme '09, Cantine Due Palme (Puglia).

PAPPARDELLE WITH DUCK AND VINSANTO: *White wine/Un vino bianco:* Sylvaner '09, Abbazia di Novacella (Alto Adige). *Red wine/Un vino rosso:* Lagrein Praepositus Riserva '07, Abbazia di Novacella (Alto Adige).

PENNE WITH TOMATO, GARLIC AND CHILLI: *White wine/Un vino bianco:* Satrico '09, Casale del Giglio (Lazio). *Red wine/Un vino rosso:* Syrah '09, Casale del Giglio (Lazio).

RIGATONI ALLA CARBONARA: *White wine/Un vino bianco:* Frascati Superiore Epos '09, Poggio Le Volpe (Lazio). *Red wine/Un vino rosso:* Baccarosso '09, Poggio Le Volpe (Lazio).

SCHIAFFONI WITH ASPARAGUS, MONKFISH AND THYME: *White wine/Un vino bianco:* Gorgo Tondo Chardonnnay '09, Duca di Castelmonte (Sicily). *Red wine/Un vino rosso:* Ulysse, Etna Rosso Doc, Duca di Castelmonte (Sicily).

PENNE WITH PECORINO CHEESE AND BLACK PEPPER: *White wine/Un vino bianco:* Antinoo '09, Casale del Giglio (Lazio).

TONNARELLI WITH GENOVESE PESTO, POTATO AND STRING BEANS: *White wine/Un vino bianco:* Riviera Ligure di Ponente Pigato '09, Terre Bianche (Liguria). *Red wine/Un vino rosso:* Dolcetto d'Alba Boschetti '08, Marchesi di Barolo (Piedmont).

Orechiette with broccoli and salsiccia: *White wine/Un vino bianco:* Santa
Caterina Chardonnay Salento '09, Cantine Due Palme (Puglia). *Red wine/Un
vino rosso:* Primitivo di Manduria Es '08, Gianfranco Fini (Puglia).

Orecchiette with artichokes: *Sparkling wine/Un vino frizzante:* Brut Spumante '09,
Garofoli (Marche). *White wine/Un vino bianco:* Antinoo '09, Casale del Giglio
(Lazio).

GNOCCHI

Gnocchi with hazelnut sauce: *White wine/Un vino bianco:* Grechetto '09 Antonelli
(Umbria). *Red wine/Un vino rosso:* Montefalco Rosso Riserva '07, Antonelli
(Umbria).

Gnocchi with porcini mushrooms and clams: *White wine/Un vino bianco:*
Verdicchio di Castelli di Jesi Podium '08, Garofali (Marche). *Rosé/Un vino rosé:*
Komaros '09, Garofali (Marche).

Gnocchi with four cheese sauce: *Sparkling wine/Un vino frizzante:* Brut
Bian'd'Bianc, Giulio Cocchi '05, Bava (Piedmont). *White wine/Un vino bianco:*
Piemonte Chardonnay '09, Bava (Piedmont).

Gnocchi with Kerry lamb ragù: *Red wine/Un vino rosso:* Barbera d'Asti Sup '07,
Nizza Piano Alto, Bava (Piedmont).

LASAGNA

Traditional lasagna: *White wine/Un vino bianco:* Satrico '09, Casale del Giglio
(Lazio). *Red wine/Un vino rosso:* Mater matuta '07, Casale del Giglio (Lazio).

Lasagna with smoked Irish salmon and spinach: *White wine/Un vino bianco:*
Sereole Soave '09 Doc, Bertani (Veneto). *Red wine/Un vino rosso:* Le Nogare '09,
Bardolino Classico Doc, Bertani (Veneto).

Lasagna with porcini mushrooms: *White wine/Un vino bianco:* Sauvignon Collio
'09, Cormons (Friuli). *Red wine/Un vino rosso:* Montefalco Rosso '09, Antonelli
(Umbria).

RISOTTO

RISOTTO WITH PRAWNS AND COURGETTES: *White wine/Un vino bianco:* Gavi di Gavi Cor de Chasse '09, Bava (Piedmont).

TUSCAN SAUSAGE AND CABBAGE RISOTTO: *Red wine/Un vino rosso:* Panzano '07, Castelli del Grevepesa (Tuscany).

MUSHROOM RISOTTO WITH PARMIGIANO PETALS: *Red wine/Un vino rosso:* Barbaresco Montefestano Riserva '05, Prodottori del Barbaresco (Piedmont).

RISOTTO WITH RED CABBAGE AND ROBIOLA CHEESE: *Red wine/Un vino rosso:* Barbera d'Asti Sup '07, Nizza Piano Alto, Bava (Piedmont).

RISOTTO WITH GRAPPA, QUAIL, SAFFRON AND RADICCHIO: *White wine/Un vino bianco:* Silvaner '09, Abbazia di Novacella '07 (Alto Adige). *Red wine/Un vino rosso:* Lagrein Praepositus Riserva, Abbazia di Novacella '07 (Alto Adige).

RISOTTO WITH CREAM OF SCAMPI: *White wine/Un vino bianco:* Naeli Vermentino di Sardegna '09, Dolianova (Sardinia).

RISOTTO WITH FRUITS OF THE SEA: *White wine/Un vino bianco:* Greco di Tufo '09 Docg, Feudi di San Gregorio (Campania).

RISOTTO WITH SCALLOPS AND FENNEL: *White wine/Un vino bianco:* Vermentino di Gallura Superiore Monteore '09, Sella & Mosca (Sardinia).

RISOTTO WITH RADICCHIO, GORGONZOLA AND WALNUTS: *White wine/Un vino bianco:* Tocai Friulano '09, Cormons (Friuli).

RISOTTO WITH BUTTERNUT SQUASH, SPECK AND GRANA TRENTINO: *White wine/Un vino bianco:* Sauvignon Collio Doc '10, Cormons (Friuli – Venezia Giulia).

RISOTTO WITH BAROLO: *Red wine/Un vino rosso:* Barolo Sarmassa '06, Marchesi di Barolo (Piedmont).

RISOTTO WITH CREAM OF ASPARAGUS AND PECORINO: *White wine/Un vino bianco:* Grechetto Poggio della Costa '09, Sergio Mottura (Lazio). *Red wine/Un vino rosso:* San Clemente '09, Castelli del Grevepesa (Tuscany).

MAINS

PAN-FRIED HAKE WITH VINE CHERRY TOMATOES: *White wine/Un vino bianco:* Antinoo '09, Casale del Giglio (Lazio). *Rosé/Un vino rosé:* Albiola '09, Casale del Giglio (Lazio).

CALAMARI FILLED WITH RICOTTA AND PISTACHIO NUTS FROM BRONTE: *Sparkling/ Un vino frizzante:* Prosecco Valdobbiadene Doc '09, Antonini Ceresa (Veneto).

SICILIAN COUSCOUS: *White wine/Un vino bianco:* Insolia '09, Susumano (Sicily). *Red wine/Un vino rosso:* Etna rosso Musmeci '08, Tenuta de Fessina (Sicily).

KING PRAWNS WITH CITRUS AND ZIBIBBO SAUCE: *White wine/Un vino bianco:* Etna bianco Pietramarina '06, Benanti (Sicily).

PARCELS OF IRISH SALMON WITH CITRUS SAUCE: *Sparkling wine/Un vino frizzante:* Brut Rost '07, Garofali (Marche).

FISH PARCELS WITH CHERRY TOMATOES, CAPERS AND OLIVES: *White wine/Un vino bianco:* Fiano di Avellino, Pietracalda '09, Feudi di San Gregorio (Campania).

SEA BASS WITH BLACK OLIVE AND POTATO CRUST: *White wine/Un vino bianco:* Valle Isarco Riesling Praepositus '08, Abbazia di Novacella (Alto Adige). *Red wine/Un vino rosso:* Kalteresee Auslese '09 Doc, Abbazia di Novacella (Alto Adige).

SQUID, PEAS AND POTATO STEW: *White wine/Un vino bianco:* Fiano d'Avellino Pietracalda '09, Feudi di San Gregorio (Campania). *Rosé/Un vino rosé:* Costa d'Amalfi Rosato '09, Marisa Cuomo, Furore (Campania).

POT-ROASTED RABBIT: *White wine/Un vino bianco:* Grechetto Poggio della Costa '09, Sergio Mottura (Lazio). *Red wine/Un vino rosso:* Montefalco Rosso Riserva '07 Antonelli (Umbria).

VEAL LIVER WITH SHALLOTS, VENETIAN STYLE: *White wine/Un vino bianco:* Sereole Soave '09 Doc, Bertani (Veneto). *Red wine/Un vino rosso:* Ognisanti Valpolicella Villa Novare '07 Doc, Bertani (Veneto).

SIENESE SAUSAGE AND BEAN CASSEROLE: *White wine/Un vino bianco:* Latour a Civitella '06, Sergio Mottura (Lazio). *Red wine/Un vino rosso:* Panzano '07, Castelli di Grevepesa (Tuscany).

TWICE-COOKED POLPETTE: *White wine/Un vino bianco:* Frascati Superiore Poggio Verde '09, Principe Pallavicini (Lazio). *Red wine/Un vino rosso:* Shiraz '08, Casale del Giglio (Lazio).

VEAL STEAKS WITH PROSCIUTTO AND SAGE: *White wine/Un vino bianco:* Orvieto '09, Sergio Mottura (Lazio). *Red wine/Un vino rosso:* Principe Pallavicini (Lazio).

CHICKEN ROULADE WITH MORTADELLA, SPINACH AND PINE NUTS: *White wine/Un vino bianco:* Gemella, Sauvignon Blanc '09, Bindella (Tuscany). *Red wine/Un vino rosso:* Morellino di Scansano '09, Grevepesa (Tuscany).

CHICKEN WITH YELLOW PEPPERS AND BLACK OLIVES: *White wine/Un vino bianco:* Grechetto '09, Antonelli (Umbria). *Red wine/Un vino rosso:* Petit Verdot, Casale del Giglio (Lazio).

BRAISED LAMB SHANKS WITH BALSAMIC AND WINE REDUCTION: *Red wine/Un vino rosso:* Barolo Canubbi '06, Michele Chiarle (Piedmont).

FILLET OF PORK WITH PORCINI AND TRUFFLE STUFFING, AND BALSAMIC REDUCTION: *Sparkling wine/Un vino frizzante:* Oro di Altalanga Doc Cuvee special, Cocchi (Piedmont). *Red wine/Un vino rosso:* Barbaresco Docg, Casa Brina Bava (Piedmont).

ROSEMARY GRILLED LAMB CUTLETS: *White wine/Un vino bianco:* Grechetto di Colle Martani '09 Doc, Antonelli (Umbria). *Red wine/Un vino rosso:* Baiocco '09, Antonelli (Umbria).

FILLET OF ORGANIC IRISH BEEF WITH RED WINE REDUCTION, PARMIGIANO PETALS AND ROCKET: *Red wine/Un vino rosso:* Brunello di Montalcino Riserva '04, Fattoria dei Barbi (Tuscany); Pannone Sagrantino '05, Antonelli (Umbria).

TRIPE WITH TOMATO, MINT AND PECORINO: *White wine/Un vino bianco:* Grillo di Sicilia '09, Antonini Ceresa (Sicily). *Red wine/Un vino rosso:* Nero d'Avola di Sicilia '09, Antonini Ceresa (Sicily).

POLENTA

POLENTA WITH MUSHROOMS AND GORGONZOLA: *White wine/Un vino bianco:* Sereole Soave '09 Doc, Bertani (Veneto). *Red wine/Un vino rosso:* Ognisanti Valpolicella Villa Novare '07 Doc, Bertani (Veneto).

POLENTA WITH ITALIAN SAUSAGE AND PORK RIBS: *Red wine/Un vino rosso:* Teroldego Rotaliano Foradori '07, Elisabetta Foradori (Trentino).

DESSERTS

TIRAMISÙ WITH VINSANTO: *Dessert wine/Un vino dolce:* Vinsanto liguoroso Clantum '07, Castelli del Grevepesa (Tuscany).

RICOTTA AND AMARENE CHERRY TART: *Dessert wine/Un vino dolce:* Stillato '07, Principe di Pallavicini (Lazio).

RICH CHOCOLATE CAKE FROM CAPRI: *Dessert wine/Un vino dolce:* Passito della Pantelleria '08, Carlo Pellegrino (Sicily).

LIMONCELLO AND PEACH CAKE: *Liquor/Un liquore:* Limoncello

PANNACOTTA WITH FRUITS OF THE FOREST: *Dessert wine/Un vino dolce:* L'Asti di Asti '09 Docg, Cochi (Piedmont).

DARK CHOCOLATE, PEAR AND RICOTTA CAKE: *Dessert wine/Un vino dolce:* Riciotta della Vapollicella Docg, Bertani '07.

CIAMBELLONE YOGHURT SPONGE CAKE: *Dessert wine/Un vino dolce:* Marsala Superiore Doc, Cantina Pellegrino '07 (Sicily).

SHORTCAKE JAM TART: *Dessert wine/Un vino dolce:* 2006 Malvasia, Pallavicini.

BISCOTTI (Vinsanto is perfect to serve with cantuccini, cat's tongue and lemon almond biscuits): *Dessert wine/Un vino dolce:* Vinsanto '07, Castelli del Grevepesa (Tuscany).

CHEESE: *Red wine/Un vino rosso:* Amarone della Valpoicella '03, Bertani (Veneto), Recioto Valpolicella Valpantena Doc, Bertani (Veneto).

Conclusion

Writing this book has given me the opportunity to reflect on fifteen years dedicated to the restaurant business. I say this because the restaurant business takes over your life, 365 days of the year, twenty-four hours each day. You are married to the restaurant. The whole family is married to the restaurant, it is all-encompassing and there is little time to reflect beyond the minutiae of day-to-day activities.

I have enjoyed retracing our steps, recalling particular moments, such as when we started our little deli in Sutton, working the till with my young daughter asleep on my shoulder, and Stefano braving freezing cold temperatures to sell Italian artisan produce at the Temple Bar market. My son Ghinlon, a young student of sixteen years of age, was responsible for the antipasti section of our new little wine bar at South Frederick Street. Seán insists that he started working at nine years of age and the girls Aislinn and Federica now admit that they used to take their friends to the storeroom to eat *biscotti* and *caramelle* (sweets).

Why did two people with four young children give up two excellent pensionable jobs to start an adventure in the food business? Why did we choose uncertainty over certainty? I have been wondering about this lately. I know we wanted a good place to raise our young family and we wanted to do something we loved. We shared a passion for Italian food and wine so it just seemed natural at that time to start a business based on what was essentially our hobby. No risk assessments were made, no business plans drawn up, no projections studied – things just unfolded on a day-to-day basis. Although we have worked extremely hard over the last fifteen years, the rewards have been many. We have met hundreds of interesting people through the restaurant and a large number of those have become our friends.

Staff are an integral part of our family restaurant and we have enjoyed working with many young people and learning from each other over the years. We are eternally grateful to everyone who has worked with us, with a particular appreciation of Stefano Baglioni and Gianmarco Raimondo, two accomplished chefs who were eager to assist me in preparing the dishes for my daughter Federica to photograph, Silvia Cittadini, who was the catalyst in getting started, Marzia and Elio who patiently corrected my Italian, and my son Ghinlon, who translated and interpreted Stefano's thoughts in the introduction. A special thanks to Mary Feehan of Mercier Press for offering me this opportunity to publish and to the wonderful staff at Mercier, especially Catherine, Wendy and Patrick.

Index